The
Baby
Mind
Reader

The
Baby
Mind
Reader

Amazing psychic stories
from the man who can
read babies' minds

DEREK OGILVIE

HARPER
element

HarperElement
An Imprint of HarperCollins*Publishers*
77–85 Fulham Palace Road
Hammersmith, London W6 8JB

The website address is www.thorsonselement.com

and *HarperElement* are trademarks of
HarperCollins*Publishers* Ltd

First published by HarperElement 2006

10 9 8 7 6 5 4 3 2 1

© Girlie Whirlie Media Ltd 2006

Derek Ogilvie asserts the moral right to be
identified as the author of this work

A catalogue record for this book is
available from the British Library

ISBN-13 978-0-00-722935-5
ISBN-10 0-00-722934-8

Printed and bound in Great Britain by
Clays Ltd, St Ives plc

To whom much is given, much is expected in return.

For Casper, Beryl and Mo, and to all who have helped me in whatever way possible, large or small, on this incredible journey.

Contents

In the beginning

I've always had an affinity with children. In fact, I don't know any other adult who gets on with children better than I do. If someone asks me my age, I tell them that I am 40 years old. Deep down though, I'm really only eight. I've always felt eight years old, apart from when I was younger than eight, when I felt my real age. Now, no matter how many birthdays I've had, I've never really grown up. I'm not Peter Pan and would never want to be. I have the body of a 40-year-old man but in my mind I know the truth: I am eight to those in the know and 40 to those who aren't. I am a child at heart and always will be.

Apart from being eight, I am also a psychic medium. I help those on the other side to communicate with the loved ones they've left behind. Actually, that's not totally true. I don't communicate with the spirit world – spirits communicate with me. I've also been talking to babies and small children telepathically for a number of years.

I know that in some people's minds this is even stranger than talking to the dead, but in many ways it's almost exactly the same. The difference is that I only occasionally see the dead, whereas I always see the children I connect with. The dead communicate with me on three levels, as do children: I can hear, see and feel the energy that both dead people and children send me. Sometimes I get a little stressed out, especially if I have a number of dead people or children talking to me at the same time. Luckily, every signal is sent to me on a different frequency so I never get confused, no matter how many babies or ghosts are in the same room! It's very much like the different stations on a radio. Sometimes these differences are rather subtle but I've grown to understand them very well over time.

I love my job and enjoy the work that I do. If someone had told me years ago, when I was running my music shop or making my million in the bar and club world, that I'd be doing what I am now, I'd have told them they were off their head. It's funny how life turns out in the end, and isn't it strange how your dreams may stay just dreams if you don't trust in them enough?

I have many memories of the hopes and dreams that I had as a child and then as a young man. Since then there have been happy and sad times, huge successes and bitter disappointments, friendships I've kindled and pals I've lost along the way. I realize that I am lucky. I haven't lost faith and am still enjoying this rollercoaster ride called life.

I'd no idea that babies and toddlers could communicate telepathically with me until I visited a young mum for a private reading in her home. Normally I would ask for there to be no distractions, but she hadn't been able to find a baby-sitter for her daughter, who was around two-and-a-half years old.

I vividly remember sitting in her flat in Glasgow. There were a couple of spirits there that I'd noticed the minute I entered her home. However, I instantly became aware that her child's psychic energy was very strong. I could feel her trying to communicate with me in a way I'd never known before. I really wanted to start talking to the spirits who were in the room but she and I immediately connected, and the images she sent to me came thick and fast. Surprisingly, I could easily picture them in my head. These images were also very easy to understand, much easier than the messages I'd sometimes get from the spirit world. I could feel the build-up of this information in the centre of my brain and I just couldn't hold back the words. I opened up and started telling her mum lots of details about her life.

'Your daughter's telling me that she loves Jaffa Cakes. She wants you to get her one from the kitchen.'

'Yes, she seems to like them. She cries for them all the time,' said the now bewildered mum. 'How on earth did you know that?'

'She also tells me that her daddy is a taxi driver and has been separated from you since your daughter was a baby.'

The little girl went on to tell me that her tummy had been sore for a few days and that she liked to go driving with her granny in the red car, although her granny smoked and always kept the front passenger window open. 'Your daughter loves the bucket and spade that her granny just bought her. She's looking forward to going to the seaside and playing with it.' All these details rolled off my tongue, just as if a spirit had told me. It was like a normal conversation, although this wasn't normal at all. No-one had uttered a word. The information had all come from this young child to me through our minds. Nothing else!

I recall the mum's reaction as if it were yesterday. She freaked! I remember having to think on my feet and panicking inside about what to do as I wanted to appear in control of the situation. I just stayed as cool as I could and quickly tried to calm her down and appease her by telling her that her child was obviously very clever. Inside, however, I was praying that this was a one-off and that this young girl was just special in some way and had a gift like mine. I knew I had to carry on with the reading in order to bring some normality back to the proceedings so I tried to contact the spirits she had initially wanted to receive messages from. Spirits did come through, thankfully, and the rest of the evening went without a hitch.

My experience with this mum and her child left a bad taste in my mouth. The last thing I wanted was to upset anyone through my work. On the way home in the car I was still pretty shocked. Was this occurrence really a one-off? Maybe I had some amazing gift that had been lying dormant for years, or perhaps I'd been ignoring another aspect of my psychic abilities. Were most babies and toddlers psychic, and if they were could they all communicate fairly easily with me?

When I think about my childhood, my mum was always around. There doesn't seem to have been a moment when she wasn't cuddling me or reassuring me that things would be all right. My mum really loved me, and I was a very lucky little boy to have someone who cared so much about my wellbeing. I love my mum and suppose I've always been a bit of a mummy's boy. Mum's been a tower of strength when I've needed her and an adviser when I sometimes didn't, but she's always been there through thick and thin, and that's been a blessing to me.

It hasn't all been a bed of roses though. Mum's been great – don't get me wrong – but she and I have had the strangest relationship over the years. Like many mothers and sons, we know how to hurt each other and how to wind each other up. Mum and I now seem to have an understanding. I think we are just beginning to come to terms with our differing personalities. It's a pity it's taken all this time.

In some ways I've always felt a disappointment to my mum. When I was a child, she'd tell me I was going to make a fine husband and dad. This made me feel bitter because I knew, even from a very early age, that this would never happen. I think that's why I'd get so angry with mum when she'd say something that upset me. I just wanted her to love me and not the person she thought I was. I felt awful about that.

I was also highly sensitive and a bit of a loner as a child. I would love just being at home, and would disappear into my own little world with my Lego set or watch *Blue Peter* on television. Mum would always get upset with me because I wasn't out playing and getting into mischief with the other boys on our street. I guess it was around that time when I started to get a bit of a chip on my shoulder about life. My attitude was 'I'm going to show everyone when I'm older that I'm as good as them.'

I was born in Paisley, Scotland, in 1965, the younger of two children. My loving sister Elaine was four years older, and very protective of me. Like any brother and sister, though, we fought like cat and dog when we were young. Elaine used to pull my hair whenever we had a fallout. To this day I blame her for my lack of thatch on top!

My dad was a heating engineer who worked for British Airways at Glasgow Airport. He has always had a wonderful work ethic and I have learnt a great deal from him. When I was a youngster, however, there were times when I didn't see dad for days or even weeks. He would come home from work, have dinner and then disappear into the night in order to plumb in someone's washing machine or sort out some problem with their central heating. Dad tells me that he never let anyone down and always turned up for a job, no matter what. If only today's workmen lived by those rules.

It would be really interesting at this point to mention that I was the son of the seventh son of a seventh son, but I wasn't. My dad did have five other brothers but he was his parent's sixth son and that, I'm afraid, is that. My dad had an Aunt Minnie, though, who was a fortune-teller. Minnie seemingly used to hold psychic nights in her house in St James's Street in Paisley and read people's tea leaves. I never met Aunt Minnie but my father assures me that she was the real deal. He told me that Aunt Minnie met with him one night when he was still courting my mum and, after the obligatory cup of tea, read his leaves. She told him that within two or three years he'd be working at Glasgow Airport and would fly all over the world with an airline. True to form she was right. I don't think I've inherited any of Aunt Minnie's gifts, though, since I'm not a fortune-teller, but I would like to have met her. I'm sure there's always a chance that she'll come through to visit me when she has the time.

I believe we are all born psychic, and we either choose to use our gifts or we don't. It's as simple as that. From day one, I always felt different from everyone else, although until I was much older I couldn't put my finger on what that difference was and what it would mean to me. When I was around nine or ten, I knew that I definitely had a sixth sense. I remember sensing things that my friends or family couldn't. Although I couldn't tell the future or what a baby or young child was thinking, I did have something. I just didn't know what my abilities were or what they really meant to me, and I never paid that much attention to them.

Around that time our elderly next-door neighbour passed away. For months afterwards I could feel his presence in my bedroom. It was then that I realized what I could sense. I could see dead people! His ghost, or what I now know to be his spirit, used to come and stand at my bedroom door when I was tucked up in bed, and he would stare at me for hours! The funny thing is that I didn't find this in the least bit scary. I just went along with it and it didn't really bother me at all. I would try to force myself not to go to sleep, just in case I missed out on getting a message from him or – more importantly for me, being someone who believed in God – instructions from what I understood to be heaven. That battle was seldom won, though, and I'd always fall asleep before anything was said! Strangely, over those few months as I fought back the tiredness, he never uttered a word to me and he never changed his expression. He just looked and smiled and that was it. He seemed to be content, though, which pleased me greatly, and no longer in any of the pain he'd experienced before he died.

My ghostly visitor left me with mixed feelings at the time. Although I was pleased that he was okay, this was tinged with a little disappointment since I felt that without some form of communication between us, no-one would believe my story. I decided not to give my parents or his family any information about him as I had no means of providing proof that he was coming through to visit me from the other side. I was also reluctant to tell people because I didn't want to appear strange or, God forbid, different. I just put this down to being me and kept my mouth shut.

Over the years my sixth sense has never left me. I've always known it was there, although I chose to ignore it many times in my life when I felt I had other, more important issues to deal with. If only I'd paid it a little more attention!

I had a fairly normal childhood. I say 'fairly' because if I am honest – which for the first time is probably now as I write this – I was never 100-per-cent happy. I always felt that I never really fitted in. I always felt different.

I didn't have a lot of friends as I never wanted to do what other boys did. Because I didn't like rough-and-tumble games I was thought of as a bit of a sissy. I was awful at football and as this was the benchmark for how cool you were, I would always be looking over my shoulder, especially at school, in case someone wanted to pick on me and have a fight.

I hated school. I just didn't want to be there, although my primary school days weren't that bad. I think this was because I felt special then. I was very clever and always excelled in maths and anything associated with music. I started playing the accordion and singing when I was eight, and from then on wanted to be on the stage or television. I believed that this was my calling. I remember making up my mind from that early age that music would be my way out of the humdrum life that everyone around me seemed to be living.

From the age of nine or ten, I began to tell anyone who asked me what I wanted to be when I grew up that I was going to be a millionaire and would make my money from being in the music business. How strange, then, that this was to be exactly what would happen. I must have been giving out psychic messages when I was a child, even though I didn't realize it at the time!

My gran has undoubtedly been the most influential person in my life. I was always very close to her. She was, and still is, a wonderful woman. Kind, considerate and the perfect hostess, she was always happy to see me or anyone who came to visit her. Since she crossed over into the spirit world six years ago, my gran has been my guiding light, and I see it as no coincidence that my talents as a psychic have soared since she passed away. I don't think that my gran is necessarily my spirit guide, though. She is watching over me and does give me advice when I need it (and sometimes when I think I don't!) but it's a common misconception that when a close relative passes away they immediately become our guide in the afterlife. Relatives and friends may come through with messages for us and be looking out for us, but that doesn't mean they are our guides or guardian angels.

When I was a youngster, my gran was very supportive and always encouraged me in whatever I did. This is still happening even now but it's being shown in a different way. It seems significant that my gran was taken from me when I most needed her to be by my side and yet she has helped me more than I could ever have dreamed of now she is in spirit. When I was a youngster, I thought I loved her, but over the years I've grown to understand that our relationship is much stronger than that. It's a bond that will never be broken.

I can now see how after-death communication is so precious to those who seek it. The connection I have with my gran is so important to me and something I really treasure.

I remember Christmas Day 1976 as clearly as if it were yesterday. Sitting at the dining table with mum and dad and the rest of the family, I started feeling very, very strange. Something inside my head just clicked and I became fully aware of everyone and everything around me. I could feel other people's pain. I could feel lots of energy, more than I'd ever been conscious of before. I became more vibrant, alert and complete. My brain seemed to have exploded and expanded, and I was suddenly aware of more than I had ever known previously. These few seconds of time were to change my life forever.

Everyone who was sitting around the table with me on that eventful Christmas Day was totally oblivious to this. They carried on eating and having a chat. However, experiencing this totally crazy event had changed me. I now felt that I was a piece of the people around me and in them. I was a piece of everything and in everything. I was still me, Derek, but I was also aware of this something else. This was something I wouldn't get to grips with for another 20 years, something I would put to sleep in my head and try to ignore until it resurfaced at the most unlikely time in my life.

During my final couple of years at primary school I became very friendly with my classmate Susan Lee and her younger brother Graeme. Graeme was eighteen months younger than me but we were around the same height and build and looked to be the same age. Graeme and I got on well and never fought or fell out. There was another boy who played in the street whose name was Eamonn and he was a year older than me. Graeme and I were inseparable during the long summer holidays. Things changed, though, when I went to secondary school and we didn't see each other much after that. Eventually we lost contact. I regret that because I really loved him.

Graeme died on 28 March 1984, when he was 17. I was 19 at the time and had just come home from college when mum gave me the news. My gran had been to visit us the previous day and had mentioned that the bus she'd been on had driven past a car accident. I hadn't given this a second thought, and would never have dreamt for one second that Graeme would be the only passenger fatally injured in that crash. His death really affected me, though I kept those feelings close to my chest. Graeme was my first love and I've never told anyone until this moment. I couldn't even tell him. I was too scared to do something like that. It was the 1970s, and being gay wasn't as accepted as it is now. I was just an 11-year-old boy confused about my feelings for my closest friend, and that was that. I kept it quiet and tried to deal with it in the best way I could. I was glad that Graeme stopped calling me when I went to high school, and we didn't see each other as often. It hurt me just to be around him because I loved him so much. I did see Graeme when it was his turn to come up to the big school. I kept my distance from him, though, because I still had feelings for him and didn't want to be friends for all the wrong reasons. I respected him too much for that.

I miss Graeme to this day and think about him. What would he be like now? Would he and I have kept in touch? Would he have a wife and family and have reached his full potential in life?

When I think about Graeme it just makes the pain of his loss all the harder to bear. Graeme's spirit has been to visit me on a few occasions, and as I write this he is by my side. He usually turns up when Eamonn and I are together, when I'm least expecting it, and sends us both messages. He loves to talk about the countless games of football and badminton we played when we were just boys. He misses those days and us as much as we miss him. He now realizes I had feelings for him and laughs about it with me, which is amazing. I loved Graeme, and although it's taken me 30 years to say it, I'm glad that I have. Those were great days and he was the best friend I ever had.

During my first couple of years at secondary school I found it very difficult to fit in. My cheery demeanour was just a front. Deep down, I hated just about every second of school life. I didn't want to tell my mum and dad or let on to anyone about my problems because I was worried what their reaction would be. I couldn't let anyone into my real world. How could I tell friends I could sense things I thought they couldn't? And, more importantly, how could I tell them I was gay? I just kept my head down and tried to get through those horrid days as quickly as possible.

No matter how hard I tried, I couldn't change how I felt about boys, and this was beginning to prove embarrassing for me at school. I would get flustered when I saw boys I liked, and found it difficult to hide these emotions.

Inside, I became very angry about my situation. From this point in my life, I became determined to be a successful person. I wanted to hit back at the world for inflicting me with this 'gay disease' and giving me a sixth sense.

Around this time I stopped sensing the spirit world. Almost immediately, I became very insecure about myself and started to worry about what people thought of me. It was difficult enough knowing I was different because I was gay, but this was exacerbated by my ability to tune in to classmates and feel their energy. By my third or fourth year, I started finding it difficult to sit in class without having panic attacks, so I started sitting at the back whenever I could to hide away from everyone. I'd got it into my head that because I could feel energy, everyone else could as well. I thought that they just dealt with it better than me, which was why they hadn't mentioned it! Looking back, all of this seems crazy, but it was my way of dealing with my issues. Deep down I knew I was on my way to having an emotional breakdown.

I was clever at school but in no way reached my full potential. I struggled through my final years of schooling, sat my exams and ended up with enough qualifications to go to the local technical college. In many ways it was decided for me that I should do an engineering degree, so in order not to upset the apple cart I applied, signed the forms and was accepted.

I hated my course. I just didn't want to be an engineer. I wanted to be a pop star and on television. The problem was that I didn't know how to go about doing this so I forced myself to go to college and get a qualification, just in case my pop career didn't take off. It wasn't to be one of my better decisions.

I didn't fit in at college from day one. I wasn't the engineering type and had no real aptitude for or interest in it. In my second year, I had what I thought was a nervous breakdown. When I initially went to the doctor and told him I was having panic attacks on the bus and hot flushes in lectures, he told me I was just going through an awkward stage in my life. He suggested I might subconsciously be finding the pressures of college life a little difficult, and struggling to come to terms with the possibility that my childhood dreams weren't going to become reality. It was all very man-to-man, 'it's time to grow up' stuff but I knew there was more to it than that. I understood the reasons better than anyone but didn't want to share them in case I was ridiculed.

I went along with the doctor's theory that the pressures of college had made me unwell. This was not a total lie because I did hate every second of it. However, the truth was that I was finding it really difficult to cope with being gay and couldn't handle lying about my sexuality any longer. Additionally, I was even more conscious of energy at that time, and could 'feel' things from people, especially my fellow students. I could sense their health problems and personal issues which, quite honestly, were sometimes a great deal more than I needed to know. I really thought I was going mad. I knew I had some sort of sixth sense but hadn't realized why I had it or, more importantly, how I should use this ability. At that time it was more of a hindrance than a blessing, and I thought I needed some professional help in order to get these crazy thoughts out of my head.

I was never honest with the psychologist who was assigned to look after me. Within the first few minutes of meeting her I realized that all she understood had been programmed into her by her profession, a profession that had a total disregard for all things psychic. I had to face reality – what I thought I needed wasn't going to come from her.

What I'd been trying to cope with was draining me every day. I was exhausted, both mentally and psychically. My nervous breakdown took its toll, and I was forced to repeat my second year at college. When I went back to college after the summer break I felt slightly better about myself. I was more confident and was beginning to come to terms with my situation, albeit in a rather weird way. I had made some decisions during the holidays. I was going to put my worries about being gay and psychic in a little box, lock it and throw away the key. I decided that the more I ignored my issues, the less they would worry me and the happier I would become. I didn't even stop to contemplate what this decision could do to me psychologically. I would pretend I was just a normal, straight guy, and this was the image I would portray to my new college buddies.

My new fellow students were very different to the ones I'd been with in my previous years. They were friendlier and more socially aware, and I quickly made friends with a group of boys who would become a great influence in my life, although I didn't know it at the time.

One summer, I was looking to make some money, and one of my college pals, John, offered to go busking with me in Glasgow. John played guitar and I accompanied him on my accordion. We both had a go at singing but after a few hours it started to rain and we tried to find somewhere to shelter. John noticed that there was a music shop nearby so we went along to have a look as he was thinking about getting a new guitar.

I hit it off immediately with the music shop owner, Peter Bryce. I suddenly realized that if I bought a few guitars out of local papers or from students at college I could clean them up and sell them on in my new-found friend's music shop, hopefully making a profit. Within a few months, after much negotiation and wheeling and dealing, The Guitar Store in Glasgow was born. I had new dreams now and knew that I had to follow them or I would be miserable for the rest of my life, so I left college during my finals, much to mum and dad's annoyance, and set my sights on being a businessman.

Doing the business

The success of my new business was astounding. I was now running The Guitar Store on a full-time basis. Within a year I'd bought out my business partner, Peter, the owner of the original shop. I put every hour God sent into making that shop work. I needed something to concentrate on so I would forget about my sexuality and dim my sixth sense. The Guitar Store flourished and I moved to new premises in Hope Street in Glasgow in 1988.

I kept working hard, building up the business over the next few years until I sold it in 1994 to a major music manufacturer and wholesaler. By that time I'd worked non-stop for seven years and was totally burnt out. I needed time off. After a protracted negotiation period, I walked away with around £200,000 from my deal and started to think about my next move. The amount wasn't anywhere near the magic million figure, but at least I was on my way to my dream.

I'd been working hard and making good money so I liked to splash the cash now and again. Looking back, I now realize this was the start of my problems with money. I had reached a stage in my life when I felt I needed money in order to be me. Money had become my God and I hadn't noticed it.

During the summer of 1994, I made the biggest decision of my life: I told the world that I was gay. It was during that time that my psychic abilities took a hold of me and soared. I think that at the moment I was honest with myself about my sexuality I just became me – the whole me, not just the pretend me who had tried for years to fit into the heterosexual world. There was no more pretence and no more lies to hide behind. I was free.

To my surprise, no-one was offended by my revelation. It was the release I needed, and in some way it helped me come to terms with the dramatic event that had taken place at the Christmas dining table all those years before.

It was then that I decided to try my luck in the bar and club world, an area of business I thought would help me achieve my childhood goal. I still wanted to be a million-aire! I bought my first bar, Mojo, for £250,000.

During my time working in Mojo I noticed that my psychic abilities as a medium started to become more pronounced. Within the first few days, it became fairly obvious to me that the building was haunted. The ghost who would come to try and talk to me seemed, from the information I managed to get from her, to be stuck there, as if she was in some sort of time warp. She was always tearful, and I knew from the emotions that would run through me when I connected with her that she needed help quickly.

I was very inexperienced at that time, so through a friend of a friend I managed to locate a medium whom I thought would be able to help me deal with my spiritual encounter. The medium was helpful but honest enough to tell me that she was also out of her depth. I therefore decided to bring in the 'heavy squad', and located a couple of Glasgow University chaps who were part of a psychic society and asked them to come and sort it out for me. They did and were incredibly helpful. After much investigation, they told me that the ghostly presence I had been tuning in to was the spirit of a prostitute who had been murdered in the early 1920s in the building, and that she had obviously been seeking help to cross over fully into the spirit world. Thankfully, she had come across me, someone whom she knew could communicate with the dead, and had just managed to get her message through. We arranged for a priest to come to the bar and bless it in order for the prostitute's spirit to be given the peace she'd been craving for nearly 80 years.

I started to see my first boyfriend, Michael, around the time I opened Mojo. Michael, a teacher, was very support-ive when I began doing psychic readings for friends and family. His encouragement really helped me come to terms with my sixth sense.

Within a year of opening Mojo, I had achieved more than I thought possible. The bar was doing great and had become one of the coolest bars in Glasgow. However, I was beginning to get itchy feet. It was therefore a great relief when, in the summer of 1996, I received a call telling me that someone wanted to buy Mojo for £620,000. I jumped at the chance.

My next bar project, Ocho, also made me a great deal of money. Because it was doing so well, in 1998 I decided to sell it and open another bar in Glasgow, Bar Budda. I'd always wanted to be a nightclub operator as it seemed a cool thing to do, and work on Budda Club started in late 1998. During the renovation of Budda Club, located above Bar Budda, we went from one crisis to another. The budgets went through the roof, but somehow we managed to open for business in late December, just in time for the Christmas and New Year period.

Michael and I were working totally opposite hours at that time. I would be going to work when he was asleep and coming home just a few hours before he was due to get up for work. This issue, along with the advent of financial worries, started to put quite a strain on our relationship, so I wasn't that surprised when Michael asked me to sleep in a separate bedroom.

By March 1999 I was beginning to panic when I noticed that the club's fortunes were not turning in the right direction. I'm not proud to say it, but I was losing my nerve. For some strange reason, I just knew that this was the beginning of the end.

Michael had bought me some books for Christmas that I'd still not read by March. One night, in order to escape from the worries of life, I decided to read Richard Branson's *Losing my Virginity*. I now wish that I hadn't. I came across a couple of very interesting chapters that I felt had been written just for my benefit. I noticed that when the Virgin empire was in financial trouble, Richard expanded his company to increase cash flow. This gave him time to reconstruct his business and keep the creditors from the door. This, I thought, would be my plan too. I'd open up a couple more bars with borrowed money from the brewers, who at that time didn't know the full extent of my financial troubles, and use the extra cash flow from those bars to pay creditors. This would also buy me time to figure out how to make the club work properly. I was excited and felt back in control again.

Initially, my plan went quite well but by August the club was not making enough money for me to pay my many creditors and also keep the bank happy. To make matters worse, the successful Budda Bar was starting to lose credibility because of its association with the rather uncool club located upstairs.

After much soul-searching, Michael and I decided to sell our beloved home and try to shore up the company with the equity from the sale. It was a terrible wrench and put a further strain on our relationship.

This was one of the most difficult periods of my life. Friends who had made a great deal of money from me over the years were deserting me by the barrowful. People I trusted didn't return my calls and, worse still, my staff began to lose respect for me. Many left and found other jobs in Glasgow's overpopulated world of bars and clubs.

Now when things are bad they can get really bad, even when you think they can't get any worse. One Friday evening in November 1999, I received a call from my lawyer, Brian. He told me I had a major problem. The liquidation accountants were on their way to the Budda Bar to close it down.

I couldn't believe what I was hearing. What the hell was going on? I knew nothing about this writ and was totally stunned. I literally dropped everything and ran out of the house. I could hardly breathe and was shaking with fear.

There were tears in my eyes and my head was bursting. If I couldn't get over to Brian's office as quickly as possible I would be out of business within the hour. I tried desperately to find a taxi but it was almost impossible at that time on a Friday. So I started running. I ran and ran through the streets of Glasgow's West End in the pouring rain. I'd been running for a good five minutes when I saw a taxi with its 'for hire' light on. Within minutes I was at Brian's office, shaking with fear and in a terrible state.

Brian told me I needed to raise £25,000 by Monday morning to prevent my business being closed down. The weird thing was that the sale of our house was due to be completed the following week, so at the back of my mind I knew that if I could borrow money from somewhere I could repay it almost immediately from our sale proceeds. I lifted the phone and called my dad. He was pretty shocked when I told him about my predicament. He wanted to help but had only around £3,000 in ready cash. If I wanted more, he would have to make some calls and get back to me. True to his word, dad called back within the hour and told me that he could get another £10,000 from a friend of his. I managed to raise the remaining £12,000 from the weekend's takings at my bars. I thought I was safe. I had bought time.

I don't know how I got through those dark days of November 1999. I suppose I just dug deep and hoped that things would turn out all right in the end. I was still fairly young and in good health, which meant that I could always start up again in business if I felt the desire to do so. But the magic was slowly disappearing from my world of wheeling and dealing and bars and clubs. I just couldn't see myself going through the trauma of starting up from scratch if my business went bust.

At this point, I found comfort in knowing that I could – if need be – take my own life. I understand that this may sound rather melodramatic or even selfish, but it was this thought and the ultimate level of control it brought me that really kept me going. No matter how bad things got, I had a get-out clause. It was also strangely comforting to know that I had an insurance policy that would pay out £1 million on my death, even if I committed suicide. If the worst came to the worst at least I'd be able to leave Michael and my family enough money for them to be fairly comfortably off.

I was constantly bombarded with calls from creditors. Unfortunately, there wasn't that much in the kitty to pay them. I could feel my business slipping away from beneath my feet like quicksand.

When we finally sold our house, it wasn't the antici-pated answer to my financial problems. Once we'd paid off our mortgage with the cash from the sale we were left with approximately £113,000. As soon as the money hit our account the bank manager used some of it to pay off my company overdraft, so we were left with £73,000. The bank manager wasn't finished though. Michael and I had credit cards, which we had been using for months to buy food and pay bills. Our card bill was sitting at £13,000 so the bank manager took our cards from us, tore them up and paid off the bill. We had £60,000 left but the bank manager still wasn't finished. By the time I'd paid off some of my debts, I was left with nothing. Not a penny, absolutely nothing. I now had no money to pay back my mum and dad and I was devastated.

Michael and I moved into our new home and were settling in. Christmas was only a few weeks away but we decided not to buy each other presents because we were totally broke and struggling to get by from day to day. I felt terrible for Michael. He'd put so much effort into our relationship and his reward was a house that was soon to be repossessed and a failed business.

I had to laugh when everyone in Budda Club started counting down the final moments of 1999. The worst year of my life was just seconds away from finishing, and what could be the most difficult year ever was just about to start. I hugged Michael. I knew that we wouldn't last the next 12 months together and I think he did too. We smiled as we held hands and watched the crowds party as the champagne corks popped and the streamers flew all around us. The club was full for once, which was an achievement in itself. I knew that this would be my last time in the place. People would be starting back at work within the next few days and credit managers would be on the phone looking for their money. What a totally crazy situation this was.

That Sunday evening I'd had enough. Budda was in chaos and I had to get away from it. I thought long and hard and decided to go to London. I wasn't planning on coming back. I remember standing on Tower Bridge one Thursday evening. I hadn't been sleeping too well and had started taking Night Nurse tablets. They seemed to dim my senses and got me through most days. I looked into the Thames and started to think about climbing onto the railing. The water seemed a long way down. I began to think about my life; all the highs and now the terrible lows. It didn't seem fair that I'd ended up with so much pain, but I told myself that life wasn't fair. I didn't care. I was on my way out of this madness. I put my foot on the railing and started to pull myself up. I managed to get one leg onto the other side when I suddenly heard a voice. It wasn't the voice of a passer-by. It was all around me, engulfing me. It was in my head but it wasn't a part of me. It was surreal.

'Go home and face the music,' this man's voice said. 'You will come through this and will grow from it. This pain will not last forever. Go home Derek.'

I looked around me but there was no-one there. I was shocked. I felt as if someone had just put their arms around me and I was being protected in some way. It was an amazing feeling. It was warm and calming and I felt consumed with love. Somebody somewhere was looking out for me, and I suddenly realized that this message was coming from a greater source than I'd ever known. If this was my guardian angel then I was going to listen to him. No question. I quickly pulled my leg back from the other side of the railing and picked up my bag. I wasn't shaking or nervous. I was almost being led away from there. So I walked back to the flat, called Michael and asked him to book me a ticket back to Glasgow.

I was tired and lonely but I'd decided to come home. I knew we didn't have much time left, and that it was a matter of months before our new house would be repossessed. I needed to salvage at least something out of this situation, even if it was only my dignity. After hearing the voice I'd realized that being in London meant that I was running away from my responsibilities.

Within a few days of my return to Glasgow, my gran died. She'd been ill for some time but her death seemed incredibly poignant to me. Was she leaving me now in order to help me out in another way?

Gran's death left me with an even greater issue. The £3,000 that mum and dad had lent me was gran's funeral money that she'd been saving up for years. Mum and dad now couldn't afford to pay for the coffin, the funeral, the lunch or a headstone. I was devastated.

I knew I had to do one final deal and do it quickly. I'd been negotiating the sale of my business for some time, but I wasn't at all happy with what I was being offered. I wanted to find some other way out of my financial mess. However, I'd reached a stage where I had no choice. On the day we buried my gran, the deal was finally agreed. I called Brian, my old lawyer, when I got back from the funeral, and his advice will stay with me forever. 'Derek, get out of Glasgow. You have upset many people and they will be coming after you. You aren't safe.'

When the business was sold its assets didn't cover all of its liabilities so it went into liquidation. As I personal guarantees to the bank, the brewers and some of my suppliers I had to sell off everything I owned to pay these outstanding debts, but it wasn't enough and I was made bankrupt by one of my creditors. Mum and dad got their £13,000 because I fought tooth and nail to make sure they did. Apart from the odd phone call, I didn't really get any hassle from the majority of my creditors after that. I think they all realized there was no point wasting any more money in legal fees as they had no chance of getting anything if the pot was empty.

During this period, my relationship with Michael continued to deteriorate. We weren't seeing eye to eye, and it was proving rather difficult for us to sit in the same room together.

I vividly remember one night in March 2000. Michael and I were asleep when I heard a loud bang on the door at around 5am. I had no idea what was going on so I quickly ran downstairs and opened the door. There on the doorstep was one of my creditors, and he didn't look all that happy. He had what appeared to be a baseball bat in his hand, and he forced his way into our home. He started screaming at me for his money and threatened to take our furniture away in the van he had outside. I explained that we had nothing and what furniture there was in the house was Michael's, but he wasn't one for reasoning with me and started hitting me with the handle of the baseball bat. I fell to the floor and screamed in pain at each blow to my head and body. By this time Michael had rushed downstairs and was trying to stop my attacker. Michael pleaded with the man to stop, and within a few minutes he left, jumped in his van and drove off. The police arrived 20 minutes later, but by this time Michael and I had decided that we weren't going to press charges. I knew who the man was and where he lived but I also realized that he was a single parent and had lost his wife just a few years earlier. The last thing he needed was a criminal record. He was angry and frustrated and I understood that. What he did was wrong but I forgave him at the time and I still do to this day.

The rest of my life just fell into place after that. Michael decided that he didn't feel safe in our home anymore and thought that he no longer loved me, so the next day he packed his bags and left. I was very confused at this point about who I was, and with my home about to be repossessed by the bank in the next few months, I didn't know where my life was going. Once Michael left, I suddenly became aware again of my amazing ability to connect with the dead. I think this was because I was now on my own and didn't have to mould my life to fit in with another person. I started to see and hear spirits but I was having trouble coping with my psychic powers. My friend Philipa knew a couple of people she thought I should meet. One was a lady called Elspeth, and the other was a chap called John who owned a hotel in Tyndrum.

Elspeth lived near Philipa in Helensburgh, so I went to see her one summer's day in 2000. Elspeth was such a warm and friendly woman that the moment we met I started to cry. I'm not sure if it was just me releasing all the hurt and pain I'd been through or if I felt something more from Elspeth. Looking back, I now realize that it was the beginning of my spiritual awakening, and that this meeting

– which was to be the first of many – would open me up to my true potential. I received something spiritual from Elspeth at that first meeting, something I'd never had from anyone else before. She seemed to be connected to me in such a strange and unfathomable way. We held hands like we were brother and sister and we chatted like we'd known each other for years.

Elspeth was a healer and I received some healing from her. In return, I gave her a reading which turned out to be very emotional for both of us. The son she'd lost as a small boy came through for her that day. He told me about his death in great detail; about the journey in the ambulance and his mother's despair as she stood by while the doctors tried to get his heart started again. I remember being so pleased that I could return to Elspeth the love she'd shown me that day. I continued to see Elspeth during that summer and still see her to this day. She has been a great help to me and will never know how much she helped me come to terms with my ability.

Philipa's friend John was also a healer. It took us ages to drive to John's hotel, which seemed to be in the middle of nowhere. John seemed like an ordinary bloke to me. He was quiet but cheery, with almost exactly the same demeanour as Elspeth. When he touched me I could feel his energy piercing my body. I really had no idea why Philipa had brought me to this man. She had mentioned something about opening me up to the spirit world but I didn't really understand.

John took us into one of the hotel's large function suites. It was empty so we had lots of space to work in. John asked me about my circumstances and I explained about the past few months of my life. He seemed to understand how difficult it had been for me, and as we spoke he held me in his arms. I felt totally at ease with John. This wasn't anything sexual. It was love like I'd never known before, and it was an amazing feeling. He truly did have healing hands. Within a few minutes, though, I began to feel rather faint. I lay down and John knelt over me. He held his hands a few inches from my stomach and I began to feel this rush of energy to that point of my body. It felt heavy and black. It was also a very negative feeling and I could sense that it was stuck there. I began to cough. I felt this energy rise through my body. It came up and up, slowly but surely, through my lungs, up to my throat. Then, as I opened my mouth, I could feel this rush of energy gushing out. I could feel the sensation of this negative, black, angry energy flying off the walls of the room. I started to scream and cry, like a child. Within seconds I had started to convulse and I was squirming and writhing all over the floor. Philipa had to help John hold me down. I started to swear. I cursed like I've never cursed before. I was scared to open my eyes in case I saw something that would frighten me, but my instinct got the better of me and I slowly opened my right eye. I couldn't believe what I saw. There were black spectres bouncing off the walls of that room, about six or seven of them. I saw large ones and small ones, and as I was now more consciously aware of what was going on, I noticed that the more I coughed and spluttered, the more of these horrible black shapes were flying out of my mouth.

John ran quickly to the windows and opened every one as fully as he could. He rushed back to me and, as he held me again, I could feel more of this black, negative energy trying to escape from my body. This was exhausting me. I'd been crying during all of this and was feeling emotionally drained.

'There is a lot more to come, Derek, a lot more,' John said. 'We can stop for a few moments and we can all have a rest. Maybe you'd like some water?' I was grateful for the break. I needed to get my head together. What the hell was going on?

'Look, what is all this about, John?' I asked.

'Derek, you are a great medium and psychic. You may not have realized it yet but you have been chosen by the spirit world as their voice, and this has been the case for all of your life. You've not been able to fully tune in to your sixth sense because your chakras – the energy points on your body that you'd use to connect with the spirit world – have been blocked by years and years of negative energy.

This energy has latched on to you because you are so sensitive. During your life you've had both happy and sad times and I guess more than your fair share of negative moments. You've consciously or unconsciously held on to the negative energy that's been around these disappointments and traumas. I really believe that you are here today because the spirit world knows that if you don't get unblocked now you never will. I'm now unblocking you. It's going to take some time – at least a couple of hours – and it's going to be awful for you, but in a short while you'll feel stronger and much more at one with yourself. You'll be able to fully develop your true psychic potential after this session. You'll, very shortly, be in the position to connect completely with the other side.'

'But John, tell me about these spectres. I can see them bouncing off the walls in this room.'

'There are positive spirits and there are negative spirits. The positive ones will come to you in order for you to communicate with them so they can send messages to their loved ones. The negative ones are a different story altogether. Some are angry spirits who possibly didn't want to die. Some may have unfinished business to attend to before they completely cross over into spirit, and that's what's bothering them. Most are upset because they can't yet move into the light, for whatever reason, and are stuck between this earth plane and the spirit plane. They have latched on to you because you are an easy target for them. They have been sucking you dry for years. Any time you've been feeling bad about yourself they have grasped on to those feelings and tried to depress you even more. They can only feed off you if you are vibrating at a very low frequency. The lower the frequency, the more depressed you'll be. It's a vicious circle.'

'Is that why people who are depressed find it hard to get out of their depressive state and feel awful about their lives?'

'Maybe. I'm not saying that everyone who's depressed is possessed in some way. No, I'm not saying that at all. I'm just saying that the more positive you are, Derek, the less chance there'll be for these negative entities to attack you and bring you down.'

'But where do these entities come from?'

'They are everywhere. They could be in your home or they could appear when you are walking down the street or at work. They seem to love nightclubs where they get off on the deep vibrations from the music and the drug and alcohol scene. They also really love pubs. They've no doubt managed to seek you out when you've had your pubs and club. You've been a prime target for them. You are very psychic and very vulnerable. You are also very sensitive so they don't need to use that much of their energy to plug into you.'

'So, it's possible that that's why I've gone bust?'

'Absolutely.' I was shocked, although it all made sense somehow. I had more questions to ask.

'So John, how is it that you can do this for me and others can't?'

'I am a healer and I use God's love to heal. These negative entities can't handle the positive energy I'm sending to your body. They are repelled by it so they have to escape.'

'Is that why you opened the window?'

'Of course. I don't want them to hang around in this hotel. They could do all kinds of mischief.'

I was astonished by John's remarks, but they seemed to ring true. It was all starting to fit into place. I was beginning to feel different, even though John had been working on me for only 20 minutes or so. I really wanted him to continue with the session. I could feel that I had a great deal more negative energy inside me and now I wanted it out. I wasn't scared. I just needed to know that this horrible nightmare that had engulfed the last 12 months of my life was nearly over.

We began, again, to cleanse my body of the negative energy I'd built up over the years. Both John and Philipa had to physically restrain me during some of my convulsions. I continued to writhe around on the floor for what seemed like hours. There were times when I started speaking in tongues, and Philipa was sent by John to get a Bible. I was screaming and choking when it became almost impossible to get these feelings out of my body. Eventually, however, and through a great deal of patience, John began to calm me, and it was soon apparent that the final pieces of energy were just moments away from leaving my body. When it was all over I felt incredible. I was exhausted, but there was an immense feeling of warmth and elation. My body felt lighter and my troubles were suddenly less significant.

Something else was also different about me. I could now see dead people more clearly than ever before. I walked into John's hotel bar and saw many spirits – not the alcoholic ones. They seemed much more approachable, as if I could communicate with them. Perhaps I wasn't such a threat to them now. I had to remember, though, that although my negative energy had all but gone I was still very vulnerable. I realized that until I grew spiritually I would never be totally free of negative energy. Until I knew exactly how to dispose of it myself, I would have to live with it, day in, day out. At least now it wasn't as significant as it had been and it wouldn't be able to hold me back from any of the goals I set myself. As far as I was concerned, this was the beginning of the rest of my life, and I was looking forward to it.

Learning to use my psychic gift

After my visit to John the healer, I regained the sensitivity I'd had as a child, and I noticed that it had developed considerably. This, in turn, helped bring my psychic abilities through. Suddenly I began to notice those shadows from the spirit world I thought had deserted me. I would talk openly and receive messages from whoever came to visit me from the other side.

I became very withdrawn. I didn't like having any company around and would tell friends and family to keep away. Physically tired and emotionally exhausted, I broke down in tears for no apparent reason on many occasions. The trauma of the bankruptcy had taken its toll. I understood that I was in trouble and tried to help myself by getting some much needed therapy. Unlike my last experience with a psychologist, when I was in my late teens, I was honest this time. These sessions did me a great deal of good.

I had only a few pounds in my pocket by this time, and with my house now days away from being taken back by the bank, a wealthy friend allowed me to live in a cottage he owned in Kilbarchan, a tiny village on the outskirts of Glasgow. Within a few weeks of moving in on my own, I knew that this was my spiritual home. I felt that the journey I'd been on for the past 35 years was destined to bring me to this place. The cottage was in a beautiful setting on a country estate, surrounded by woodlands. I would spend hours walking around the estate, looking at the wonderful plants and animals. I felt so lucky to have the time to sit by the lake and contemplate my future, and for the first time in around five or six years I began to relax. I became a vegetarian and started to appreciate the simple things in life. I gave up tea and coffee and stopped drinking alcohol. I began to appreciate nature and became an ardent supporter of animal rights.

Once I'd started to relax it became easier to focus on the psychic side of my life. I could see and feel things I hadn't noticed for months. I'd regularly tune in to the energy of people whom I'd sit next to on a bus or stand beside in a queue or in a shop. I'd have hours of fun connecting with their energy, finding out what was troubling them or the ailments they had. You'd be amazed at how many people have piles! I'd quickly sense what was bothering them then try to listen in to their conversations to find out if I was correct or not. It was the best fun I'd had in years, and the great thing about it was that it was free and literally on my doorstep.

My favourite game was to find a pregnant woman, perhaps in a shop or on a bus, and try to connect with her and find out if she was expecting a boy or a girl. Although I didn't realize it at the time, this was my first foray into connecting with a child on a psychic level. I took this a little too far one day whilst I was in Mothercare buying a gift for a friend's baby boy. A woman was standing very close to me looking at a little blue top, and I overheard her talking to her friend.

'I'd love to buy this for my baby, Susan,' she said, 'but I'm scared that if I do it'll be the wrong colour.'

I just couldn't resist so I butted in.

'Do you not know the sex of your baby then?' I asked, knowing full well what sex the baby was.

'No. I'm waiting for a surprise.'

'Well, I won't spoil your surprise, but I'm certain that if you buy that top you won't need to exchange it.' You should have seen the look she gave me. It was priceless!

I also started connecting with the spirits of those who had passed away. During my first months in the cottage I regularly saw the spirits of dead people. Although this may sound strange, these sightings brought me a great deal of comfort. It was as if I had found my inner self and was completing myself when I opened up and communicated with the spirit world.

My psychic calling came in January 2001. After signing on the dole for five months I was beginning to get some hassle from the benefits office about finding a job. I hadn't been looking for work as I felt that something would turn up for me. It was no surprise, therefore, when my gran's spirit came to me one day and told me that I should give myself a shake, get positive about my life and my abilities and get my own radio show. I'd known that gran was watching over me because I could feel her presence in the cottage most nights.

I'd never been on the radio before so I was slightly apprehensive about putting myself forward for what could be a total catastrophe. I felt, though, that my gran wouldn't tell me to do something that would hurt or embarrass me, so I got out my Yellow Pages and looked up radio stations. I called Scott FM and spoke to their controller, Jay Crawford. 'Look Derek,' he said. 'I'm a bit of a sceptic so you'll have to do something to really impress me.'

'That's okay, Jay. Is there anything I could say that would offend you in any way?'

'Nothing at all will offend me, Derek. Just you go ahead.'

'Okay Jay. Firstly, when I tune in to your voice vibrations I'm being told that you are getting a new car in the next few days, a blue one. There is also something coming through about you being embarrassed when you've been intimate with a lady friend.'

'That's enough, Derek!' interrupted Jay nervously. 'Call Dougie Jackson at Qfm, our sister station, and tell him I think you should be on air.'

And that was that!

Qfm was a small, homely station, and the people who worked there were very friendly. The minute I walked in I felt good about the place. When I met Dougie, he asked me to demonstrate my psychic abilities to him. Dougie sat down beside me and I started to connect with his voice vibrations. The spirit who was standing by his side started to come through to me. I was a little nervous by this point but I concentrated and began to tune in. I needed this job badly.

'I keep getting shown that you are doing work in your back garden at the moment, Dougie. When I connect with and acknowledge the elderly lady who's standing behind you, this message is very strong, very powerful. She keeps telling me that you have messed up that work, if I can be honest with you.'

'Tell me more,' said Dougie. He seemed intrigued.

'Well, it's the way you've set your garden out, Dougie. It's ended up being a nightmare for you. I gather that you'll now have to move a tree, and that a pathway has been laid in the wrong place. The opinion I'm getting through from the spirit world is that you'll have to start the work again in order to get it right. Oh, and your gran, Dougie, she says hello.'

'That's impressive.'

'And your radio station is haunted, Dougie.' I was now on a roll. 'There are loads of spirits walking about in here. It's like a busy high street. Some look as if they are lost. It's rather strange.'

'It's amazing how you've come up with that, Derek. Do you know what this building we are standing in used to be before it became a radio station?'

'No, I haven't a clue Dougie.'

'It used to be a morgue!'

I got the job.

The first time I went on air, the DJ asked me some questions about my life as a psychic medium. The more I spoke, the more relaxed I felt. Soon we had our first caller: 'Hello, hello is Derek there? I'm looking for a reading from the psychic on your show. I think he's called Derek.'

I could sense immediately that the lady on the phone had a gentleman from the spirit world watching over her.

He wasn't that difficult to connect with, which was a blessing. My gran must have been watching over me as she said she would! I just closed my eyes, as I sometimes do during readings, and tried to tune in to the caller's voice vibrations.

'Hello,' I said. 'Now you've no doubt been listening to me talking about how this works. It's important therefore that you tell me very little about yourself. As you've no doubt heard, I am a medium and I tune in to voice vibrations so in order for me to be able to help you I'd like to ask you your name, just your name. Could you tell me your name please and say it slowly to me?'

'Hello, Derek. My name is Mary.'

By buying myself that little bit of time I could now fully connect with the spirit who was there. Now I say 'there' not to describe how far away that spirit was. I'm just using it to explain that when I connect through voice vibrations the energy I tune in to is actually beside me. So the spirit I was connecting with was actually 'there' beside me in the sound booth of the radio station! Immediately, the spirit showed me the letter 'J' for James.

'Hello Mary, thanks for calling. Now you're my first ever reading on radio so I'm a little nervous.'

'So am I.'

'Okay, then let's just take this slowly. There is a man coming through to me when I connect with your voice vibrations and he keeps showing me the letter "J".'

'That may be my dad, although I'm not sure. It could really be anyone.'

'Hang on a minute. The name James is important here, and before you jump to conclusions, I'm not talking about your son. This man is covered in black soot, and he's carrying a coal bag.'

'That's amazing! My son is called James but my late father was also called James and he was a coalman!'

'Well, your dad says hello and wants you to know that he's watching over you and your family.'

'Thank you so much, Derek. That's just what I wanted to hear!'

'Now he's telling me that he passed away with a heart or chest problem. I can't quite make that out. All I'm getting is a pain in my chest but I'm sure you'll realize what he's trying to say to me.'

'My dad had a heart attack, Derek. Spot on.' Mary seemed happy that I'd completely validated that the spirit of her late father had come through to her.

'Well, he tells me that he's not in any pain now but he's been worrying about you. You must look after yourself a bit better. That's your message. Thanks for calling, Mary.'

I was on my way! The first reading of the first show and it was fabulous.

The show was going really well and the calls just kept on coming. About two hours in, I was given a note saying that the next caller on line one was Margaret.

'Hello,' said line one. 'Is the psychic there?'

'Hello Margaret,' I said.

'Oh, my God!' came the reply. 'You are bloody psychic! My pal heard you on the radio tonight and told me to call in. She said that you were amazing and you really are! How on earth did you know my name?'

'The producer of the show gave it to me on a card, Margaret, before you came on air,' I said, and we all fell about laughing!

So I passed my test and *Psychic Sunday*, my new radio show, was born.

I was starting to be a bit of a local celebrity. People weren't exactly stopping me in the street but my name was becoming well known. I started getting fan mail at Qfm, but not all of it was positive. There was the odd piece of hate mail, which was upsetting. Some people called me a fake, whilst the so-called religious ones claimed I was the Antichrist! Now, I'd be the first to admit that what I do may seem bizarre or downright spooky to the uninitiated, but I'm certainly no con man. I am totally and utterly genuine and my gift is God-given. I'd never dream of duping the public, especially those who've just lost a loved one or are in need of some spiritual guidance. Those who come to me aren't stupid either. They may be looking for something that even I can't give them, but the vast majority know when I've managed to tune in to the spirit of their loved one. They'd know if I was a liar, and I'd be a fool to think that I wouldn't be found out if I wasn't genuine.

So what can I be doing wrong? I'm only talking to people in spirit who are desperate to contact their loved ones, and to inform us in general of the realities of life. That's all. I don't connect with the dead. They connect with me. I would never dream of trying to unsettle a spirit who didn't wish to communicate. If spirits wish to send messages they are more than welcome to use me as their messenger and I will always be available to them for that purpose.

My success on the radio brought me many admirers and I received hundreds of requests for private readings. I'd made it a rule from day one that I wouldn't do consultations in my own home. It wasn't that I didn't want people to come over to the cottage; it's just that my privacy was important to me. There was also another, more psychic, reason for my decision. I knew that if I gave any form of reading at home – especially one which led to a connection with the spirit world – my inner sanctum could possibly end up full of wayward spirits.

I could switch my abilities on and off. I knew the place in my head where I needed to go in order to switch myself on and connect with the spirit world. However, there was the odd spirit out there who knew how to get in touch with me when I least expected it!

I'm not really in the habit of switching on my abilities when I'm going about my usual daily business. I tend to go into psychic mode only when the time is right and not when I'm around the general public – that's unless I'm bored or want to have some fun! I use the fruit shop in the village nearly every day, and within a few weeks of moving into the cottage I'd got to know the staff quite well. One morning, I was suddenly aware of a spirit standing in the corner of the shop. This took me by surprise because I hadn't switched on and gone into psychic mode and I therefore wasn't expecting any visitations from the spirit world. This man was adamant that I communicate with him. I was slightly taken aback by this because, being new to the village, I didn't want to create problems for myself. Even at that early stage of my life as a psychic I understood that not everyone is fully appreciative of my abilities and how I use them. I knew I had to tread carefully.

'Excuse me,' I said. 'I'm sorry to bother you.' The lady who was serving looked over and acknowledged me.

'Hello. What can I do for you today?' Luckily the shop was empty at the time so I felt confident enough to be honest with her without either getting embarrassed or causing offence.

'I'm Derek and I'm new to the village. I know that you don't really know me but I'm a medium.'

'Oh, that's interesting. I don't think we've had a medium in the shop before. By the way I'm Caroline. It's nice to meet you.'

'It's nice to meet you too, Caroline. Some people think that psychic stuff is a load of nonsense but I get the impression that you may be a believer?'

'Well, it interests me. Have you got something to tell me?'

'What I'm going to say may upset or surprise you. There is a spirit standing over there beside that double socket and he keeps telling me that it's dangerous and you're not to use it.'

'Really? Do you know who this man is?'

'I'm certain that it's your dad, Caroline. He is scared that you'll get a shock from that double socket, the one that's located just beside the onions.'

'Well, that's pretty amazing because one of the sockets on that wall doesn't work and I've been told by Billy the owner never to use it. Is my dad telling you anything about himself?'

'No, unfortunately he's not, Caroline. He is okay and he's watching over you but he's really worried about you using any one of those sockets, not just the one that's broken.'

'Well, I'll keep that in mind,' answered Caroline, and that was that.

Two weeks later I was in the fruit shop when Billy Fullerton, the owner, was there.

'Derek,' he said. 'I want to have a word with you. Did you tell Caroline not to use that socket over there because her dad's spirit told you to warn her about it?'

'Yes, I did, Billy.' I was intrigued, but also slightly worried that I'd said something out of turn. I hoped Caroline hadn't been giving her boss hassle about dodgy electrical fittings.

'Well, Derek, she didn't listen to you and decided to plug in the Hoover one night when she was tidying up. She thought it would be okay to use the other socket that was still working but for some reason it shorted out the Hoover and blew a fuse. She was lucky that she didn't get a nasty one. She nearly electrocuted herself!'

After a few weeks on the radio, I started thinking about the possibility of doing theatre shows. I felt that if I could connect with the spirit world down a telephone line whilst dealing with the pressure of being live on radio, then I'd be able to handle a theatre audience. In the meantime, I continued to give private readings.

As I didn't have a car, I used a local taxi company to take me from reading to reading. Matt was my main driver. He was a gentleman and very supportive of me and my abilities. Matt had just split up from his wife Lesley. He had three children and still saw his kids and Lesley regularly. 'I'd like you to meet the wife,' Matt said one night when we were driving back from one of my readings. 'I've been telling her all about you and she's really fascinated by what you do. Could you see her this week?'

'No problem, Matt,' I replied. 'It's the least I can do. You've been very good to me.' I don't like doing readings for people I know, but I couldn't let Matt down.

Lesley had arranged for her sister and some of her friends to be at the reading so there were a few anxious women in her flat when I arrived. Matt introduced me to Lesley and then went off to work. I went to the loo to get some privacy and took a few moments to get into the zone, to go to the place in my head where I can connect with the spirit world. I change when this happens. I become aware of energy and I can sometimes get rather agitated and fidgety. I've just accepted these traits over the years. The methods I now use to connect with the spirit world have developed over time. The more experienced I've become, the more I've mastered them, so much so that I can now jump to and from my spiritual focal point with ease.

Almost immediately, I realized that I wasn't comfortable with the energy in Lesley's flat. I suddenly became aware that there was a presence there, and it was very strong. I could feel it clearly as I stood there, anxiously, in her bathroom. I knew that it was very close to me but was unsure where. I focused and tried to work out in my head where it was.

After a few seconds I connected with it. It was through the wall of the bathroom in her hallway, standing just a matter of feet away from me, and I felt very unsettled by it. I could sense that it was powerful, and when I focused on the energy surrounding it and emanating from it, it was very black and negative. I wasn't sure if it was the spirit of a man or a woman but whatever it was, it was a presence that didn't want to talk to me. It seemed to be the defiant spirit of someone stuck in some sort of middle ground who couldn't, for whatever reason, fully cross over into the spirit world. It was angry about its predicament and it wanted me to understand that. I knew for sure that it also wanted me to know that it was there and watching me but there wasn't going to be any other form of communication between us. I was disappointed because I really wanted to make contact. I knew from my experiences of meeting spirits like these who are 'stuck' that the readings are usually very precise and last for hours.

I tried to compose myself. The last thing I wanted to do was scare anyone. I came out of the bathroom knowing for sure that Lesley wasn't going to get a reading that night and that I'd have to come back and see her on another occasion when she was on her own. I felt that the presence did want to talk to her but not while so many people were around. It obviously had something to say to Lesley that would be personal and possibly life-changing, something for her ears only.

Lesley seemed pleased to see me when I arrived on her doorstep a few days later. She'd obviously forgiven me for letting her down. I was glad to see her and hoped that her visitor would come through for her, and that her reading would go well. I wasn't to be disappointed because almost as soon as I entered her hallway it was there waiting. It was standing beside the bathroom, watching me. This time, though, I could just about make out the outline of a young man. He was in his early 30s but he wasn't particularly good at showing himself to me. Maybe his talents lay elsewhere.

I sat down in the living room and decided to come clean with Lesley. 'You have a presence in your home,

Lesley. There is someone here who would really like to talk to you. It's a man in his 30s. I'm not sure when or how he died, or even if he's a relation of yours. He may even be connected to this flat in some way. I'll try and ask him later if he used to live here, but he has a couple of messages for you and I think you should listen to them. I have to be honest and tell you that he was here the other night. I could feel his presence in your hallway but it wasn't his time to come through for you. That's why I've come back to see you today. I'm going to connect with him now and see what he has to say.'

'Okay,' said Lesley. 'Tell me what's troubling him.' She seemed eager to start the reading and who could blame her!

I tuned in to the presence, which was now standing beside me in the living room. He started instantly to tell me some details about Lesley's private life. 'He keeps telling me that he wants to shake you,' I said. 'He wants to shake you so that he has your attention. He tells me that you need to wake up and smell the coffee! I'm also getting bad vibes about your body language. You seem to be a person who is very enclosed. You need to open up more and enjoy your life. It's important.'

'Okay,' said Lesley. I now had her full attention.

'I'm being told about the shortcomings in your charac-ter and your present situation so that you listen to the main point of this. I'm sorry if this feels like a personal annihilation. Please remember this is not in any way my opinion.' I was concerned that Lesley might think I was trying to hurt her feelings. 'I'm being shown that you are currently having a relationship with someone whose name begins with the letter "D".' There was silence from Lesley. 'You must stop seeing this person. He is so boring!' I added, then burst out laughing. I could feel that Lesley knew exactly what I was talking about and that her friend, Mr D, was really boring. He was driving the presence nuts with his lack of personality and conversation. There was a serious side to the reading, though. 'The relationship must end,' I added. 'The presence tells me that this person comes over to this flat and that must also stop. Your life is going nowhere with this guy. You need someone who is exciting!'

'Oh my God, that's spot on, Derek. I'm seeing a chap at the moment called David. We've just started going out! That makes total sense.' She seemed shocked. With that revelation the atmosphere in the room seemed to change instantly. I'd said what I'd been told to say and given Lesley the correct messages. I felt relieved and suddenly very calm and relaxed. It was as if a weight had been lifted from around me. I hoped, that by sending us the messages he had, the presence would now cross over completely into the spirit world since his work was done.

Lesley and I needed a break so she went off to make some coffee and compose herself. She needed to take in fully what she had been told. We chatted for a while. She told me she was a singer and actress: 'In fact, I'm currently rehearsing *Educating Rita* with the Buddie Magic Theatre Company, but we've had a few problems and it looks like we'll have to cancel the dates. The only real worry is that we're going to lose our theatre hire deposit, and we can't really afford to do that.'

'Where were you planning on having the show?' I asked.

'We've booked a couple of nights at the Paisley Arts Centre,' replied Lesley. 'It's a pity those nights will now go to waste. They're really good nights too, in May.'

I couldn't believe my luck. I had come to give Lesley a reading and ended up with the possibility of a couple of theatre dates. As I made my way home on the bus, I knew deep down that I'd soon be appearing live on stage. I felt uplifted. I had been rewarded for all my efforts, especially all the readings I'd done for nothing and all the help I'd given those I'd met. Maybe things were starting to fall into place for me. Perhaps my new life as a psychic was my destiny.

My first psychic show

I'd no idea how to put a psychic show together. Never having been a member of a psychic group or to a psychic show before, I really didn't know what I was doing. Luckily, colleagues from the radio station helped me out with the technical side – sound, lighting and music. They also advised me just to do what I did on the radio show, to walk on stage, pick out some people – or let the spirits do that for me – and go with the flow.

I couldn't believe it when, a few days later, I called the box office at the Arts Centre and was told that both of my theatre shows had nearly sold out. I was offered another date and accepted it. I was going to be doing three nights on the trot! This meant that around 500 people would be coming to see me live on stage. I was over the moon.

I was a bit apprehensive about asking my mum and dad to come along. Something inside my head told me to let mum come but not dad. I couldn't explain why, but I just didn't want dad in the audience. When I chatted to him about it he was fine, but to this day dad's never been to see any of my theatre shows. He's had plenty of opportunity but has never mentioned it to me again. Maybe he's in a huff! Sorry dad!

It was great to see so many friends there on my first night at Paisley Arts Centre. Loads of people came backstage to wish me all the best. Although I was nervous I knew that if I kept my focus it would go just fine. When the music started my heart was pounding. 'Ladies and gentlemen, please welcome, live on stage, Derek Ogilvie.' I was on.

It took me a few minutes to find my feet. It felt strange to be greeted by applause and the startlingly bright lights, but surprisingly it also felt stimulating, exciting and exhilarating. I could feel the presence of countless spirits whirling around the theatre. They were everywhere: in the rafters, standing beside their loved ones in the audience or sitting on their knees, and even crowding around me on the stage. It was like nothing I'd ever experienced before. It was pandemonium.

There were old and middle-aged spirits, young adults and children as well as baby spirits. I could see them as blurry outlines. Many had been in the spirit world for years while others had passed away recently. There seemed to be few rules. Some hadn't continued to grow older in spirit so were coming through to me at the age they were when they passed away. Others, though, had continued to grow older in the spirit world. Some came through to me at an age at which they'd be more easily recognized by their loved ones, rather than the age at which they'd passed away. It was fascinating, astounding and downright spooky all at the same time!

Luckily, though, they didn't all want my attention. Some just said hello to me and then disappeared, as it obviously wasn't their time to come through. Some wanted to give messages to their earth-bound families and friends so I asked them politely to wait in a queue because I wouldn't be able to speak to everyone at once. I knew that if I did then the show would end up being just a rabble and I would get mixed up. One or two spirits were less than willing to wait in a queue, and bombarded me constantly with messages in order to make their presence felt. Eventually, I got to the point where I just had to do as they said or I wouldn't have been able to continue with the show without being repeatedly interrupted.

I can't remember every reading from that particular show. When I'm on stage I've got so much to remember that recalling every reading would be impossible. I'm not sure what other psychics do but I've always got a hundred things going on in my head at any one time when I'm on stage. I have to be all things to all people. I'm constantly thinking about how many readings I've done, about being entertaining and also about being understanding and sympathetic to both the spirit world and those who've been picked out for a message. I'm thinking about the readings and the messages as well as the emotional state of the person getting the reading. I'm also constantly work-ing on the quality of the connection between the spirit and myself. My biggest fear is being halfway through a reading when the spirit just goes, disappears, and doesn't finish off their message. When that happens it's a night-mare. You've just got to go on to the next reading and hope that the previous spirit comes back and finishes off what they had to say.

I have to listen to countless spirits who are continually popping in and out of my head during shows. Some infu-riate me by telling me their names and then flying off without any other form of communication. Some tell me who they want to speak to and then won't tell me where that particular person is sitting in the audience. So what do I do? I have to ask to have the lights up, if they aren't already, and request a show of hands until I find who I'm looking for. The worst thing is being told a couple of names with no other information. What do you do when you're told that James is looking to say hello to Margaret who's in the audience tonight, and when you ask for Margaret, 100 women who've lost a James put up their hands! It's usually not until I've embarrassed myself getting to that point that the spirit then tells me the all-important messages and it all comes together. We find Margaret by a process of elimination and then, when she's been picked out, tell her messages that are mind-blowing. It's amazing!

A couple of readings that occurred in my first few shows at the Arts Centre were very memorable. On the first or second night I'd noticed an elderly gentleman in the second or third row of the audience and felt the need to talk to him. There was an elderly lady by his side whom I assumed was his wife, but just behind his row and at his left shoulder was the spirit of an elderly lady. This lady was fairly difficult to connect with. Although she had made her presence felt, there was very little communication between her and me. She did do something rather strange, though, and to this day I've never had any spirit copy this technique. She showed me a red flower coming out of the gentleman's head. That was it. No other information; not a name or an indication of who she was or how she'd passed away, just this flower – and it was protruding out of the top of his nut!

I acknowledged the gentleman and walked over to where he was sitting. 'Now I know this may sound strange, but there is an elderly lady by your side. It's rather difficult to connect with her so you may have to help me along here if that's okay.'

'Oh, that's no problem. I can help you with that.'

'When did she die?'

'She's not dead! She's sitting here beside me!' The audience fell about in hysterics.

'No, I don't mean that lady,' I said, as I pointed to his companion and fought back the laughter. 'I'm a psychic, remember, I talk to dead people! I'm talking about the elderly lady who's standing beside your left shoulder, the lady who's passed away!'

'I've no idea who that could be. Can you get a name for me?'

'No, that's the problem. She won't talk to me. It's very difficult to communicate with her. That's why I need your help. Can you help me out with this?'

'Okay.' At last, I was on the same wavelength as him. That had only taken five minutes. This was a nightmare!

'Right,' I said. 'When I look at you there is a flower coming out of your head. I think it's a red flower but I'm not too sure. I may need a little more time to work that out.' I went back to the spirit world and the lady showed me what appeared to be a rose or carnation. 'Now, can you tell me anything about your connection between what appears to be an elderly lady and a flower, possibly a rose or carnation?'

'No, I can't.'

'Okay then, we're going to have to work through this one, no matter how long it takes,' I said, wondering if this reading would take over the whole show. 'I'm not being allowed to let this one go because this spirit wants to send you a message. She will not let me move on with the show. Let's take this easy so we understand each other. Have you just taken a red flower to an elderly lady's grave?'

'No.'

'Okay. Have you just planted some memorial bush or trimmed one, or maybe cut a red flower from a favourite plant in the garden recently, and that's what this elderly lady is trying to tell me?'

'No.'

'Let's look at it so far. You don't have an elderly relative in the spirit world who was a lady?'

'Yes I do! I have loads of them but I don't know which one you are talking about. I need a name or something.'

'Okay, I understand your frustrations. I'm feeling them too. This lady is obviously very conscious of telling me about this flower so that's important to her. You'll need to think here. What could this connection be?'

And then the penny dropped. His wife hit him in the stomach and said, 'You stupid bugger, your mum was called ROSE!'

'Oh, and your mum is watching over you and says hello,' I added, and quickly moved on!

That reading taught me a very valuable lesson, which is why I'll never forget it. I was taught that night that I must never give up if I get stuck on a piece of information whilst communicating with the spirit world or, as I do today, whilst talking to babies and young children tele-pathically. I've now learnt to take my time in situations like that, and slowly work through what I've already been told. This helps me to qualify the meaning in the message and to understand it more clearly.

There are times to laugh and times to cry at shows. Many babies and young children come through to speak to their mums and dads in the audience, and we also hear from older sons and daughters as well as husbands, wives and grandparents. My shows can be an emotional rollercoaster, and they knock me out emotionally and sometimes physically. I find it very hard to relax after a show. It takes me hours to come down from the buzz. Sometimes spirits follow me home from the theatre, and it's always very difficult to ask them to leave or, more importantly, to shut up. I call them Klingons! I'm glad I live in the country and that my neighbours are at a distance because I'm sure if they were in earshot they'd be very upset with me watching television at three or four o'clock in the morning, or my constant vacuuming as I try desperately to burn off the excess energy I've accumulated during a theatre show. I'm also certain they wouldn't appreciate me talking to some wayward spirits in the early hours!

I've been astounded by some of the reactions I've received from audience members over the years. There have been some very funny instances. One night, I was appearing in Johnstone Town Hall and I picked out a young woman in the audience. 'I sense from those who are watching over you in the spirit world that you've got some energy blockages in your chakras,' I said.

'Is that right?' she replied, as her face went a bright shade of red.

'Yes, you seem to have a blockage in your genital chakra. Those who are watching over you in spirit seem to think you need to sort that out. I'm sure you'll understand what I'm saying to you.' I would have continued but I wanted to save the girl's blushes.

'Well,' she replied, looking at me rather sheepishly. 'I came to one of your other theatre shows a few months ago and you picked me out and told me I had a blockage in my genital chakra, and I've had an itchy fanny ever since!'

A similar reading occurred one night when I picked out a young lady in the audience whom I felt was suffering from migraines. 'The spirit who is watching over you tonight tells me that you have a serious blockage in your third eye,' I said. 'I gather therefore that you suffer a great deal from headaches, and I've to tell you that your loved one in the spirit world knows only too well about that.'

'Yes, I do suffer from severe headaches,' came the answer. 'But I don't understand how you could tell me that.'

'Well, you've got a blockage in your third eye. I can sense it from here. I can feel your pain in the middle of my head. It's very sore.'

'But, how can that be? How can I have a blockage in my third eye? I thought only MEN had third eyes!'

When I'm in full flow during a theatre show I sometimes have to watch myself so that I don't overstep the mark or, as some may put it, the line of decency. This is sometimes difficult for me because our loved ones in the spirit world seem to take great delight in letting me in on the most bizarre secrets about people's private lives. When I'm totally in the zone, I'm miles away from my normal daily thoughts, worries or fears and I seem to lose all sense of perspective, so under these conditions my inhibitions just go right out the window. It's uncanny.

I was on stage one night when I noticed a lady sitting in the back row of the theatre. It was a small auditorium so she wasn't that far away from me. I could feel that her father was watching over her and that he wanted to say hello and send her some messages. I tried to tune in to this man's spirit, and within a few seconds he began to communicate with me. The reading was going well until I got ever so slightly stuck. I just couldn't understand what I was being shown so I had to stop for a moment and try to work out the picture in my mind.

'I just can't make out what your dad is trying to tell me,' I said. 'What I'm being shown is quite comical but I don't want to embarrass you in any way. I can stop your reading now and see you after the show or I could continue if you are okay with it.'

'I'm okay with you continuing. I'm interested now in what you have to say.'

'Well, he keeps showing me your bare bottom and it looks to me that you are sitting on spaghetti, for some reason or other.'

'Really,' replied the lady, who now appeared rather shocked. 'I have no idea what you are talking about.'

I then noticed a teenage boy sitting next to this lady getting very embarrassed and his face turning bright red. He seemed to be squirming in his seat. I got the distinct impression that he knew exactly what I was talking about and that he was just preparing himself for the revelation.

'Oh, I know what you are talking about now,' replied the lady. 'I had to think about what you were describing for a few moments but I understand what you are being told.' We all waited with bated breath. It was like a Jerry Springer show just before the guest announces their special secret. 'It's not spaghetti that you are being shown on my bum, IT'S WORMS. I'VE GOT WORMS!' We all fell about. I'd honestly never seen or heard an audience reaction like that one before. People were in hysterics. I could also see that some of the audience sitting beside this lady were trying to move away from her. They must have thought it was catching. It was so funny!

'Oh, don't worry, they're only ringworms!' she announced. 'I caught them from my friend's cat. They're all over my bare bum. They aren't really worms, though, it's just a skin complaint but it does look like spaghetti I suppose!'

Getting into print

I couldn't believe it when I got a call from the editor of the *Paisley Daily Express*, offering me a weekly psychic column. The deal was that I would answer letters sent in by readers. I knew that this could only be good for my career.

Writing my weekly psychic column was hard work initially. Every week I received hundreds of requests from readers looking to get in touch with their loved ones in the spirit world. Some of the letters were very sad: parents who'd lost children; families who hadn't had the chance to say goodbye to loved ones because of family breakdowns or squabbles.

Some of the letters I picked out changed lives. I remember hearing from a Paisley couple who were desperate to make contact with their son. I was really sure I could help them but felt I had to meet with them to connect fully with his spirit. I called them and arranged to pop over to their home.

When I met with Jim and his wife I could see they were really nervous. They were obviously desperate to hear from their son. I knew they needed some message from him to validate that he was okay and watching over them. I really wanted to help them, and thankfully it wasn't long before I made the initial contact.

'Your son is here,' I said. 'He's by my side. He tells me that he passed away after having cancer and he wants you to know that he is still tired but he's recovering well now that he is in spirit.'

'Thank you,' said Jim. 'That is what we wanted to hear.'

'It's strange but when I connect with his spiritual energy he keeps showing me a picture in my third eye of the Pope. All I can see is the Pope.'

'That's amazing,' replied Jim. 'Our son was called John Paul. I suppose he's realized that by showing you the Pope he can tell you what his name is.'

'He's watching over you and your family and also his brother. There is something coming through about his brother going to the army.'

'Yes, his brother is thinking about the army as a career,' replied Jim.

'Well, he seems to be sorry that he fought with his brother when they were youngsters. I suppose all brothers do that but to validate this a bit more John Paul tells me that his brother's not been studying for his exams and has been lying to you. I'm sure that John Paul is still trying to have a go at his brother, even though he is in the spirit world now!'

Jim and his wife seemed grateful and relieved that John Paul came through with some messages that night. I knew that by making the effort to visit them I had achieved something good for all the family, and had brought them some closure.

I really enjoyed my time at the *Paisley Daily Express*. It was wonderful to receive the countless thank-you letters from readers who'd got messages through from their loved ones in the spirit world. At that time I really thought that things were on the up. I had my own radio show, a weekly newspaper column and my theatre shows were regularly sold out. However, I'd been writing for the paper for only a month when I received some really bad news. Part of the radio network that included Qfm was bought by Real Radio. Within weeks, the implications for Qfm were clear. The station had to stand on its own two feet and to do that cost money. When I got a call to tell me that my next show would be my last I was devastated but not surprised. It was explained to me that *Psychic Sunday* was just too costly for the station to produce, and it also seemingly didn't fit in with the station's proposed new mainstream image. It was a sad day when I said my final goodbyes to my listeners in radio land and *Psychic Sunday* crossed over to the great radio station in the sky.

I vividly recall doing a psychic show soon after losing my radio job. I'd been anxious about selling enough tickets without being able to advertise the show on the radio, but with a bit of creative marketing and lots of help from my friends, I'd managed to almost fill the large auditorium of the Mitchell Theatre.

While I was introducing the show, I overheard two women in the front row having a chat. 'He's gorgeous,' one said to the other. 'I bet he's gay. All the good looking guys are.'

'No, he's not gay,' said the other. 'He's straight. Yes, he's definitely straight.'

'No, you're wrong, he's gay. Look at him. He is gay, I tell you.'

'No, he's straight. He's straight.'

This chatter went on constantly during my introduction and it wasn't stopping. 'Look, you two in the front row,' I said, in my usual cheeky manner. 'I AM GAY. Okay, I AM GAY! Now shut up. I've got a show to do!' Well, you should have seen their faces. They were so embarrassed! The audience was in stitches and soon the two women in the front row also saw the funny side and began to laugh along. When I looked over at them during the show I got the impression that they had no idea how I could have heard them from where I was up on stage. To this day I'm sure they still think I can read people's minds because not one word was spoken between them for the rest of the night!

I can also recall giving a reading that night to a lady sitting in the middle of the theatre. Her reading was fabulous and was going so well that I'm sure some of the audience must have thought it was a set-up.

'Thank you for allowing me to give you a reading tonight,' I said.

'My reading was great and I've got a great deal out of it. Thank you for coming to me,' she replied.

'Yes, it was so good some people probably think you are an actress and this has all been rehearsed.'

'But I am. I'm on the television all the time! I'm on the Scottish soap *Take the High Road.*'

My second night at the Mitchell Theatre was a whole new ball game. The minute I went out on stage I could sense I was in for a difficult night. There didn't seem to be that many spirits around waiting for me, and the atmosphere was just awful.

I was probably not on top form either. Looking back, I had been wasting too much energy before the show thinking about ticket sales. To make matters worse, the audience didn't seem that desperate to connect with their loved ones in the spirit world that evening. I honestly thought that Jeremy Beadle was hiding somewhere and would pop out at any second. It was like pulling teeth and I hated every second of it.

'Your dad's here, and has come through to say hello,' I remember saying to someone I'd picked out in the audience.

'But I don't want my dad. I want my mum,' came the reply.

What can you do in a situation like that? You just can't win!

I also recall saying to someone that I wasn't sure if it was her dad or her uncle who was watching over her so I needed a bit of help.

'I think I've got your dad here but I'm not that sure. Can I ask you, has your dad passed away?'

'Maybe,' was the reply!

Where do you go from there? Anyone who gives a response like that is just taking the piss and shouldn't be at a show. They have no respect and are treating the whole thing like a charade. It really upsets me when people act like this when I'm doing my best for them. If any member of my audience does that to me now, I move on, if I'm allowed to by the spirit world. After a very good put-down of course!

I learnt some valuable lessons that night. Looking back, I'm really grateful for the experience. At the time, though, I thought that it would be my last show and my career was finished. When you do a show you are in the hands of the 'big man' upstairs. Now, I don't really want to bring God into this, but speaking to the spirit world is all about God. Ultimately, it's up to Him if and when our loved ones in the spirit world come through, so it's not really my fault if they don't. It's also very important, if and when you get a reading, to be supportive of the medium. Obviously, don't feed them information but try to help them out if they get stuck. If you don't then the spirit who's come through with messages for you may get a little disillusioned and will disappear if it feels you're not being receptive or respectful enough.

My cousin Gerry had his own video production company. As I was keen to break into television, I asked him to film a promotional video of me giving readings in front of a live audience and also for people in their own homes.

We recorded my video, *Connections*, in front of a live audience, and Gerry hand-picked a few people for private readings. I had heard of Margaret McGhee through someone I'd met whilst doing a private reading. They had asked me to get in touch with this lady because the circumstances behind her bereavement were so tragic. When I called Margaret I understood that her son Stephen had passed away. Seemingly he was quite young and there were question marks surrounding his death.

When I arrived at their home to do the filming I was slightly nervous as it's never easy dealing with the loss of a child. I was lucky, though, because as soon as I sat down with Margaret and her daughter, Donna, I could feel that a number of spirits were in the room and had been waiting for me.

'Stephen is telling me about a name change. He is showing me the letter "M". He is trying to tell me either that his surname became his middle name or that he should have been allocated a middle name beginning with that letter. There is also a strong image coming through of a gravestone.'

'Yes, that's correct,' Margaret replied. 'I changed the name on Stephen's gravestone.' I didn't ask Margaret why she had done this but I could see from her reaction that it obviously meant a great deal to her.

'Stephen also keeps talking to me about a stereo system that needed to be repaired and was kept in your lounge.'

Margaret nodded. She totally understood what I was talking about.

'He's also telling me to turn the volume up because he wants to dance,' I added. 'He just told me that if you turned the volume down he would turn it up again the minute you left the room.'

'Yes, that's very true, he was always doing that.'

I looked at her daughter, Donna. 'Your brother just told me to talk to you about your breast! I'm sorry if this is embarrassing for you but he'd like me to continue. Is that okay?'

'Yes,' said Donna.

'There's some issue about your breast. I'm not sure what it means though. I think it's to do with bra size or cup size. Do you understand me? Is this about you trying to buy a bra that didn't fit properly or have you been getting pains in your breast caused by an incorrect bra size?'

Donna laughed nervously. 'She knows what you are talking about,' said Margaret.

This was obviously private so I decided to move on with the reading. It wasn't unusual for a younger brother to come through from the spirit world and talk to his older sister about things like this. Your personality doesn't change when you cross over into the spirit world so this brother was still trying to wind his sister up.

'Am I embarrassing you here?' I asked.

'You aren't half,' Donna replied.

'Stephen wants to talk to you about some people who are important to him. He wants to make contact with someone whose name begins with the letter "P". I'm unsure if this is Paul. This is someone your son played with, one of his close friends. I can tell you that this person seems to have passed away. They are in the spirit world with your son.'

'Yes, I know who it is,' said Margaret. 'It's my mum. Her name is Pamela.'

'My gran and I were close but she wasn't someone who would go out and kick a ball with me.'

'My mum would.'

'There are a lot of aches and pains around your mum. This is her acknowledging what she went through before she passed away. She is sending me back pain and joint pain and telling me it's a blessing that she doesn't have this pain now she is in the spirit world. She's also telling me about your feet swelling up? Do you understand this?'

'No,' Margaret replied.

'Your mum wants to rub your ankles. She seems to know that you've had a great deal of pain there.'

'I don't have any problems with my ankles or feet though.'

'Yes you do,' countered Donna. 'Remember your blood infection?'

'Ah yes, that's correct,' Margaret said.

'Your mum tells me that it seems to be your right ankle rather than your left.'

'That's correct.'

'She tells me that she's not very happy with you. There is a message coming through about separation and divorce. She feels that you didn't give a relationship a chance. I'm being told that the number eight is significant here. I feel that it's a previous relationship. Were you with the gentleman for eight years or is it eight years since you split from him?'

'It was eight years ago that we split.'

'Stephen has come back through again. He sends you his love but there are a couple of other things I'd like to say. First, when I connect with his spirit, Stephen tells me that before he passed away he had a sore head. I also feel dizzy when I'm around his spirit.'

'Stephen died after drinking a bottle of vodka he'd found lying in some bushes,' said Margaret. 'He got very drunk that night and I took him to the hospital because he started choking. They did a brain scan and told me there was something wrong with his brain. I really blame myself for his death.'

'Stephen doesn't blame you so you must get that idea out of your head right now. He's come through to you because he loves you. He isn't in any pain now and wants you to know that.'

'Thank you,' replied Margaret.

Stephen pulled his energy back at this point. He had said all that he was going to say. It had been a very powerful reading. Margaret and Donna had both got a great deal from it, as I had too.

When we were filming the promotional video at the theatre, I noticed a lady sitting in the back row of the audience. I could sense how nervous she was. She had two spirits by her side, both of whom had messages for her, so I decided to connect with them. Once I'd tuned in, I realized that one was the spirit of her husband whilst the other was a little boy who kept saying 'David' to me. The husband had his own agenda, though, and was first to speak to me.

'Your husband's spirit is here and I have to tell you that he isn't too pleased with you. I get the impression that you've been using a credit or bank card. He doesn't want you to use these cards.'

'Yes, my husband wasn't the type of person who used cards. I've got them now but he would never have one.'

'I don't want to scare you but your husband's spirit is so strong that I'm going to tell you the PIN number of one of your cards. Are you ready?'

'Yes,' replied the lady. I could sense that she was shaking with fear.

'Okay, there's something coming through about four then six. Do you understand that?'

'Well, I'm a little nervous.'

'Are the first two numbers four and then six?'

'No, they are the second and third numbers.'

'That means that the first number is one. So the numbers are one, four, six and the final number is seven I think. It's definitely a high number but it's not coming through too well. I'm sure it is seven but it could also be eight or nine.'

'The PIN code is one, four, six and seven,' she replied.

'Thank you. Your husband says hello!'

Everyone in the audience was stunned.

'There is a little boy with you. He's come through from the spirit world to say hello and he keeps saying the name "David" to me,' I continued.

'I'm not sure about that.'

I felt that I might be crossing the line and didn't want to go any further but the spirit world was telling me to keep going. 'Look, your husband's got a little baby boy with him in the spirit world and he wants you to know about that. David seems to be another son I think. Do you understand that?'

'Well I understand David being a son.' Then she decided to open up to me. 'I had a miscarriage just after I got married.' She was shaking and her top lip began to tremble. I knew I'd hit a nerve and I felt awful. This was obviously something that had been hidden away and not discussed for years. For some reason, though, I had been told to push this point with her. Maybe it was her husband's way of letting her know that her baby was now safe with him. I just hoped that when she got home and thought about her messages she understood why they had come through to her in this way.

There was a pregnant lady in the audience that night. She was in the front row and I noticed her immediately. The spirit standing by her side sent me strong messages of warmth and wellbeing, and I therefore felt the need to connect with her. 'I have a lady here who tells me there's been an accident. Someone was in a car and had a smash.' I looked at the girl intently.

'I had a smash last year,' she replied nervously. 'I wasn't injured or anything.'

'That's okay, no-one said that you were. I'm being told that you've been worried about wearing your seat belt because you are pregnant.'

'That's correct. I have been concerned about it.'

'She's telling me that you wished you didn't have to wear your seat belt because if you had another accident you'd injure your baby.'

'Yes, I worry about that all the time.'

'It's important, therefore, that you get your brakes fixed on your car. There is also something wrong with your radio. You're obviously being watched when you're out driving!'

'My brakes make a strange noise, especially when I'm driving in the wet, and my radio is broken. I'll have them both looked at.'

'Now I'm being told the sex of your child. Would you like to know that?'

'Yes.'

'You are having a boy,' I replied. 'Were you hoping for a boy?'

'Yes,' she smiled.

'I want to validate that further so you will believe me. I'll tell you something that only your close family know.' I went back to the spirit world. 'I'm being told that your son's due date is very close to another relevant family date. It's within a day or so of something important.'

'It's my dad's birthday the next day.'

'The spirit world wants you to know that they think it would be wonderful if your son was born on the same day as his grandfather.'

'My whole family were just talking about that. I would love for that to happen.'

Part of my job description, I guess, is having to deal with unhappy events. It's one of the down sides of my work. Many of the most difficult readings I've encountered are to do with suicides and murders. I have worked with the police on a couple of murder investigations in and around Glasgow. In 2003, I was contacted by the mother of murdered schoolgirl Caroline Glachan. I was able to get lots of information and had two meetings with the police. I've also had my fair share of unnatural deaths to handle.

I went to visit a family in Johnstone during the making of the video. When I got to the house I was greeted by three sisters and a lady I assumed was their mother. It became rather clear within moments of entering their home that their brother's spirit was there waiting for me. He was in the spirit world with an elderly gentleman who seemed to be his father, as they had a strong family connection, but I wasn't sure. We all sat down and I began to tune in to them.

The brother immediately told me that he had passed away in rather unusual circumstances but wouldn't say what they were. I told the rest of the family that I could feel there was a great deal of emotion in the room. 'First of all, I'd like to ask if there's anyone here who would not wish me to get personal with them if particularly sensitive information comes through in this reading?' Everyone seemed to be fine with this so I knew I could continue openly and freely. 'Okay, there are two spirits here at the moment. One is a father figure and the other is a young man. The father figure has also lost a brother to the spirit world. Is your dad still with us?'

'Yes, he is, but we have lost two uncles. Our mum's brothers,' replied one of the sisters.

'That's correct,' said mum. 'I've got two brothers in the spirit world.'

'There is a young man with them. I feel that he is your son.' I looked across at mum and she smiled. 'There is so much emotion around his energy that it's quite unsettling for me to tune in to him at the moment. I have to tell you that there seems to have been a great deal of confusion around him before he passed away. When I tune in to his spirit I can feel my head spinning, and there is a tremendous pain in my heart and chest. It's as if my lungs want to burst. He's trying to tell me that he overdosed on something and his heart gave up.'

'Yes, we fully understand this. That's my son.'

'He wants you to know that there is a little boy with him. I feel that this little boy is his nephew. I get the impression from this tiny spirit that he crossed over into spirit when his mum had a miscarriage when she was around two months pregnant.'

'I was about six to eight weeks gone when I miscarried,' replied one of the sisters who was sitting directly in front of me. She was shocked and started to cry. One of her sisters put her arms round her.

'Well take some comfort from knowing that your son is now with your brother, although I have to tell you that there is also a little girl with them. She's just come through to me to say hello.'

'I've no idea about that,' the sister replied.

'This girl is older. She tells me that she was miscarried at four months.'

'That'll be my daughter,' said one of the other sisters, her voice wavering with emotion. 'I miscarried at four months.'

'Let me validate that.' I went back to the spirit world and asked this young girl for more information. 'I've just been shown a ring. What she's telling me is that you've had a problem in your relationship with her father and you've separated from him.'

'Yes, that's correct,' she said, holding tightly to her sister's hands.

'The more I connect with your brother, the more I want to vomit,' I exclaimed. 'He's swallowed something and trying to fight back. I'm getting extreme blockages in my throat and my lungs are bursting. This has happened all at once. He's been confused and felt let down before he passed away. He's telling me that a partner of his let him down badly. He feels cold and isolated. He will not tell me what happened to him though.'

'He died after inhaling fumes from the exhaust of his car,' replied one of the sisters. All three sisters and their mother were very tearful by this stage.

'Looking back now,' I continued, 'he wishes he hadn't committed suicide. He's so embarrassed that he gave in. He's telling me that he could now cope easily with his problems.'

The finished video looked really good. I sent out at least a couple of dozen tapes to all sorts of people in the television industry. One Friday evening I was totally shocked to receive a call from a production company. They'd seen my tape and wanted to talk to me about the possibility of working on a new show for Living TV called *Scream Team*. This was amazing news!

The basic premise behind *Scream Team* was simple. It was based on the cartoon *Scooby Doo*, brought to life with a real gang of ghost-busting kids! The production team auditioned six young people, and planned to scare them to bits by sending them to the most haunted or potentially psychic areas of Britain.

I'd been asked to meet with the 'team' at Hope Animal Rescue Centre, outside Darlington. Filming would begin almost immediately, so my first television appearance was going to be an outside broadcast in the middle of a park with animals walking around freely. My job was not simple. I was asked to tune in to the spirit of a mutilated wallaby. Once I'd connected with it, I was to find out what injuries it had sustained during its final moments and, if possible, ascertain who or what had killed it. They weren't asking for much then!

I was obviously nervous but tried to stay as calm as possible and concentrate on the job in hand. I'd thought about how I would handle this situation and felt that I'd just do what I normally did when communicating with the spirits of dead people. This, I believed, would be my best chance of tuning in to the wallaby's spirit.

I could feel the tension in the air when I began to compose myself. I was conscious of the cameras and sound man needing to pick up from me exactly what was happening so I talked through each emotion and tried to describe it as fully and accurately as I could. Surprisingly, I managed to get into the zone quite quickly, and after only a few seconds I could sense the presence of the wallaby's spirit. It was then that the information began to flow. I could sense a great deal of pain in my right shoulder. It was as if someone were trying to cut my arm off. I could then feel my arm being torn from its socket and the blood oozing from my body. I suddenly got a pain at the bottom of my spine. I could sense someone tugging at me and trying to pull the skin from that area of my back. I knew that if I'd had a tail then it would definitely have been dislocated in some way but I wasn't sure how.

The next sensation was even worse. My neck became tight and I struggled to get my breath. I could feel the sinews in my neck being pulled and tugged. My head started spinning and then I had the most unbelievable sensation of all – my head was pulled from my body and then cut violently from my neck. This all happened in a few moments. I felt that the attack wasn't random. It had been planned. I could feel the presence of many men around me as the attack was taking place, and in the distance I saw a man standing on the roof of a white van. Within a few seconds of this amazing information coming through, it was all over. I lost the connection and the wallaby's spirit was gone. The Scream Team and the camera crew just stared at me in wonder.

I was aware that any information I'd brought through from the spirit world had to be backed up, so I was pleased to hear that the body of the wallaby was in deep storage and would be examined later in order to verify my psychic connection. After dinner we were all taken to the veterinary hospital where the crew had arranged for us to meet a vet who was going to carry out the autopsy on the wallaby.

I'd never seen a dead wallaby before, or in fact any animal that had been in cold storage for a while, and it wasn't the prettiest sight in the world. I'm very squeamish so I didn't last long in the operating theatre. It was fascinating, though, because the minute the body was shown to us I knew I'd got most of the messages correct! The head and right arm were both missing. The head had been ripped from the body and the remaining tissue had been severed through the neck. The arm had been cut off at the shoulder. It seemed, though, that the tail was intact, and that this area of the body hadn't been touched in the attack. For a few moments I was concerned that this part of my account wouldn't be validated.

'Derek, you got everything correct so far,' said the surgeon. 'I'm now going to cut the skin back around the tail and see what condition it's in.' Everyone held their breath.

'Oh, my God,' said one of the Team. 'The skin's bruised at the base of the tail where it connects with the body. How on earth could Derek have known that?'

The production company were so impressed that they immediately asked me to do the next *Scream Team* show, which was going to be in Edinburgh. I was fascinated by the goings-on in and around Mary King's Close. The Close, located in the heart of Edinburgh's old town, had been used in the 17th and 18th centuries, mostly by the working-class citizens who lived and worked there. When the plague hit Edinburgh in the 18th century, the residents who became ill were forced to stay in the 'Vaults' under the street, and both the entrance and exit were closed up in order to keep the population under tight scrutiny.

I'd been told that there had been many ghostly sightings in the Close, and also a great deal of poltergeist activity. I am fortunate enough to be both clairvoyant and 'clairaudient' so I can not only see dead people but hear them as well. Many spirits, though, are very resourceful and will communicate in other ways.

When I arrived, the Team were already inside the Vaults, waiting for me. I was met outside by one of the production crew. We said hello and talked about what we were going to do that evening, but within a few seconds of meeting her I was seized by a huge reluctance to enter the building. Although it was August, and a beautiful summer's night, I felt cold and started to shiver. I then noticed the presence of a young man standing by my side. I was suddenly filled with a deep sense of foreboding. This panicked me as I'd never before felt energy like this from a spirit. I could feel that the man was in his late 20s, and I noticed that blood was dripping from his throat and chest. He was angry and seemed on edge. I was conscious that he was in some sort of turmoil, but he was trying to beckon me away from the entrance to the Close, which scared me.

I told the crew about what was happening, and that I wasn't so sure now about doing the show. They seemed totally perplexed. Without me there was no television show. What were they going to do if I didn't even enter the building? But I had other things on my mind. By this stage my heart was pounding and I'd started to cry. I broke down, sobbing openly in the middle of the street. I was engulfed by all manner of emotions. It was like being the ball in a game of tennis, being hit from one extreme to another. Looking back at the footage from that night, I feel slightly embarrassed by my reactions but it all happened so quickly that I didn't really have time to think through what I was doing. In those first few seconds of connecting with that spirit I'd completely lost control of my own feelings and was at his mercy.

I decided that I needed to get away so, without thinking, I ran down the street, trying somehow to disconnect myself from this rogue spirit who was trying to attach himself to me. I kept running until I was out of sight of all the crew. I just needed some time to calm down and compose myself and to contemplate my next move.

I knew that I had to return to the Vaults. I couldn't let the production company down. I decided, against my better judgement, to go back and face the spirit who was unsettling me. I hoped that when I settled down and perhaps spoke with him I'd find out what was actually troubling him, then maybe – just maybe – I could help him to move on in some way. This was a long shot as I'd never been in this position before. I was in for a bigger shock when I returned to the spot. My rogue spirit had gone. I was mystified. What had happened to him? Why had he come through? Did he know something I didn't or, worse still, was this a warning? There were so many questions but I had to be realistic. The clock was ticking and I had a stressed-out director looking frantically at me.

I decided to go for it and began my walk down the long, dark stairway. As soon as I entered the Vaults I heard a man's voice. He was shouting at me and I felt him push me out of the door. 'GET OUT. GET OUT!' I nearly wet myself! I looked at the cameraman's face and noticed that he wasn't in the least bit upset. Had he not heard anything? 'I've just been told to get out,' I said. 'Someone is also pushing me. It seems pretty serious. I'm not sure if I can continue.'

I was worried. I'd had a few spirits possess me in the past and it wasn't an enjoyable experience. The last thing I wanted was for a spirit to be so upset with me that it entered my body and tried to attach itself to me. However, I knew that I had to keep going. I pushed myself to go further into the Vaults. On the stairway, two spirit girls brushed past me, both in their early teens with blonde hair and dressed in 18th-century attire. I was surprised but not shocked as they didn't react negatively to me. They knew I was there because one moved over to allow me to walk between them. The one on my left was slightly smaller than the other but I was taller than both of them. One was laughing whilst the other didn't look too happy at all. I could feel the sensation of cold air flowing through me as they went past. I remember shivering. I wasn't scared but it was a weird experience and it kept me on my guard.

At the foot of this long and winding stairway I was greeted by a man, not one of the crew but a gentleman from the spirit world! He was older than me, in his mid-50s. He looked at me and I turned away. I wanted to avoid eye contact. I just knew that if we acknowledged one another, I could be in trouble and I didn't want to take any unnecessary risks. I walked through into the main area of the Close, to where the Team were waiting for me. I was glad to see them but concerned too, as I could immediately feel the presence of a little boy running about my feet and tugging at my trousers. 'Can anyone feel anything?' I asked.

'Yes,' replied Shaylla, one of the Scream Team. 'Someone's been pulling my hair.'

'Yes, there is a little boy here. He is very mischievous. He wants to let you all know that he likes to play with the visitors who come into these Vaults. I can hear the name Jimmy.'

We walked around the Vaults for half an hour or so, during which I could feel lots of spiritual energy, but after a while I became rather disillusioned. It seemed to me that without validation, without knowing the history of the Vaults and who lived there, anyone could say just about anything about the place. Any so-called psychic could mention that there was a spirit standing in a corner or that they could hear voices.

I wanted to find out if my psychic connections matched with the history of the Vaults. Luckily, Fran Hollingrake, a local historian, was helping out that night. I went through some of my stronger experiences with her to see if they fitted with any of the stories she'd heard previously from other psychics. She validated that there was a guy at the front door who says 'Get out!', and that there was a little boy who pulls your hair and tries to make mischief. She was also familiar with the aggressive chap who had pushed me out of the front door.

'And there is a kid buried in that wall!' I'd kept my final piece of information until the end. After I'd said it there was silence from the crew and a couple of the Team screamed. I knew I'd hit a raw nerve.

'Yes, it's a wee girl who's buried there!' replied Fran.

I'd been worried by the lack of validation but thankfully, through Fran, I was vindicated. My readings had been accurate and I was pleased with the outcome.

Receiving a message from the spirit world can be a life-changing event. There are times when I'm so adamant I'm right about the message that I'll argue with someone if I have to. I remember picking out a gentleman from the audience at one of my shows. His dad had passed away and had a few messages for him.

'Your dad tells me he was taken away in an ambulance. He was very ill and wants you to know that he is now free from pain and watching over you.'

'Thank you.'

'Now he wants you to know that he's with your brother. Please let your mum know that.'

'But I don't have a brother, Derek.'

'Look, I'm being told that your dad's with your brother and that's the message I've to give you.'

'But I don't have a brother so that can't be right. You've got this wrong somewhere, Derek.'

'You have a brother in the spirit world. Maybe you should ask your mum about it.'

'Okay, I will.'

A few days later I got a call telling me that the chap went home that night and called his mother. She told him that before he was born she'd given birth to a stillborn baby boy, who was buried in the same graveyard as his father.

I vividly remember giving another reading to a gentleman and his wife. His granny had come through and I could validate her presence really well. 'I've got your granny here and she's stinking of fish and chips. It's really smelly!'

'Granny loved fish and chips. They were her favourite food.'

'Your granny tells me that she's got the budgie with her and it's now safe.'

'Oh, that'll be Joey. He died years ago!'

At this point the audience were in fits of laughter, and who could blame them? In all my years of giving readings it seemed unbelievable that a spirit would come through and talk about a budgie, but she had and I therefore had to send that message through to her loved ones. 'Yes, I'm being shown that budgie right now by your granny. It's a lovely blue colour.'

'No, Joey was green. He was definitely a green budgie.'

'No, I have to tell you that your message is that your granny is looking after the blue budgie.'

'Thank you for the message but the budgie was green.'

'Look, I really don't want to be calling you a liar, but the budgie I'm being shown is blue and that's the truth of it.' I was beginning to get slightly frustrated by that point so I moved on with the rest of the show.

Do you know that I heard a few days later that the chap went home after the show that night and found his blue budgie lying dead in its cage! Sometimes the truth is stranger than fiction.

By now I'd appeared at the Paisley Arts Centre around 20 times. All my shows at the venue had sold out, and each time I arranged another one the tickets would be gone within a few days. This was my bread and butter. I needed to do these shows to pay the rent. I was on stage one night and picked out a lady, whom I got to know later as Pauline Kerr. Pauline was sitting at the end of a row so I went over and sat on the step beside her.

I'm not a fortune-teller, but if I'm told to tell someone something then I will. Yes, I may cushion the blow if it's bad news but I will always tell the truth and do the job that the spirit world requires me to do. 'I can smell gas when I look at you,' I said. 'I'm being told that you've to look out for gas.'

'But I don't have gas,' replied Pauline.

'Listen to the message.' I touched Pauline on the arm. 'Legs 11!' I exclaimed. 'Legs 11! I'm being told that you are going to go to bingo and win on legs 11.'

'Well, that's good to know.' I knew from her answer that she didn't believe me so I asked the spirit world for more information.

'Look, Pauline, don't dismiss this message. I know it sounds far-fetched. When you go to bingo you've to buy four cards. You'll win on the fourth card and the winning number will be 11.'

I received a call from Norman at the *Paisley Daily*

Express office the following Tuesday. He told me he'd been contacted by Pauline. She'd been to bingo and won £800 on the number 11 on her fourth card! Not only that, but her next-door neighbour had had a gas leak at the week-end. Norman was impressed and wanted to do a feature on it. I wasn't in the least bit surprised by this news. Spirits can help us out in the most unlikely situations, some of which can be life-changing.

Becoming a baby mind reader

After my first experience of communicating telepathically with a child, I continued to do private readings and started to come into contact with more babies. I'd ask parents to let their babies and young children stay in the room during the reading so I could try and tune in to them. Some would talk to me but others didn't want to know and wouldn't utter a word. I wasn't fazed by this because I knew some spirits didn't want to talk to me either.

I got a call from a woman called Arlene McDougal who lived in Dumbarton. Arlene explained that she was desperate to get in touch with her mum who had passed away four years earlier, so I agreed to see her.

Like many mums, Arlene had her baby with her when I entered her house. I got the impression that her husband was going to take the baby upstairs whilst I was in their home but I really felt the need to let the baby stay with his mum. I was sure he was going to communicate with me.

As soon as I started to get myself into the zone I began to connect with her three-week-old baby, Morgan. Morgan's energy was absolutely amazing and it was really easy to communicate with him. I began to get excited because the information was coming thick and fast.

'Your baby tells me that you have cut a nail too far down on one of his fingers,' I said as I sat down beside Morgan and Arlene.

'No I didn't!' said Arlene. Then she looked and was amazed. There was a small cut on the top of Morgan's index finger! For a moment she gave me a stare which was priceless. 'How on earth did you know that?'

'Well, believe it or not I can talk to babies telepathically. I know you've invited me here to get a few messages through from your mum, and I will try and talk to her spirit in a few minutes, but at the moment I'd like to continue communicating with Morgan, if that's okay?'

'Okay, but I just can't believe this. It's amazing that you can talk to Morgan!' Arlene was obviously taken aback by what I'd just said but I really wanted to continue with the reading. I didn't want Morgan to get tired and for the reading to finish abruptly. Morgan's connection with me was still strong and I could feel lots more messages coming through. 'Morgan tells me that you've moved his Moses basket around the opposite way so you can see him better. You've also changed the side of the bed you normally sleep on so you can now look at Morgan when you're lying there.'

'I still can't believe what you are telling me. That's totally true.'

'Morgan doesn't like the fact that you don't always heat his bottles up during his night feed, Arlene. He prefers the way his dad does it. He likes his milk warm as cold milk gives him a headache.'

'Yes, I've noticed how he's different when his dad feeds him. I'd no idea why that was.'

But there was more. 'Morgan also tells me that you've just changed the light bulb in the bedroom because you thought it was too bright for him. It was, so you did the right thing. Well done! You've also just changed Morgan's cot mattress.'

By this time Arlene was dumbfounded. She was just sitting looking at me, then Morgan and then her husband, who was sitting on the couch open-mouthed.

'It's weird,' I continued, 'but Morgan tells me you thought you were having a girl and that you would have called her Rebecca. He also tells me that your husband's big toenail is missing, and there's something coming through about Morgan's grandfather having a sore leg and being off work with an injured finger.'

By this time both Arlene and her husband were getting used to what was happening and were starting to enjoy it. 'You're totally correct in what you're telling us, Derek,' said Arlene. 'I'm amazed that Morgan knows these details but he must be picking up on what's going on around him.'

Morgan then showed me a picture in my head of what appeared to be a very large building. I immediately understood what he was trying to say to me. 'Morgan tells me that you are just out of hospital and that you've been through a great deal lately. Your son wants you to know that he loves you both. Watch what you think about and say in front of Morgan. He's listening to every word!'

Arlene and her husband looked so pleased that Morgan had spoken to me. They seemed shocked, of course, but they trusted me and realized I was actually communicating with their son. I went back to Morgan to find out if he had anything more to say but the connection had gone. He was obviously tired so dad took him upstairs so that I could continue with the reading. 'Your mum's also here with me tonight,' I said.

'That's great,' said Arlene. 'I really wanted to hear from her, even if it's only for a few moments.'

'She wants you to know that she's been watching over Morgan. She has a few messages for you though.'

'Thank you,' said Arlene. I could sense that she was getting rather emotional about this whole thing and I really couldn't blame her. I was also finding it difficult to take in what had been happening since I'd arrived.

'You have a shoebox in the cupboard with things belonging to your mum inside. There is a newspaper cutting in this box. This is your mum's way of validating that she is here for you and watching over you tonight.'

'That's really amazing,' said Arlene. 'No-one knows about that box or what's in it apart from me. That really confirms that mum is here with Morgan and me. Thank you for coming, Derek. This whole thing has been amazing. Thank you so much.'

When I left their house after the reading I was ecstatic. This baby thing was really coming together for me, and it wasn't just a coincidence. It was pretty obvious to me that many babies had this ability. Babies could communicate telepathically if the conditions were right and they had something to say. Maybe I could now help children who had greater issues than Morgan had with his bottle. Perhaps I could help children with medical problems or sleeping, eating or crying issues. I had to let the world know that I could talk to babies.

As my reputation as a baby mind reader started to grow, more and more mums asked me for help with their children. I've been amazed at some of the things children tell me. I was once with a little girl called Abbey whose mum, Aileen Gallagher, had got in touch. Aileen was worried that one-week-old Abbey was unwell. She'd repeatedly asked her health visitor about Abbey's breathing but her pleas were falling on deaf ears.

When I arrived at Aileen's house I immediately connected with her daughter, but her messages were not what we both expected. 'Abbey tells me you've bought a new white leather sofa,' I said.

'No, my mother-in-law's just bought it. It's being delivered soon. I was just talking to her about it before you came over tonight. Abbey's obviously getting confused somewhere along the line.'

'Yes, maybe she is. Sometimes that can happen.' I was interested, though, in Abbey's breathing. I could hear her wheezing in her cot and it wasn't the most pleasant sound. I tried to tune in to Abbey fully. I had to work hard. It was difficult to understand what she was trying to tell me and, not being a medical practitioner, I didn't want to come away with the wrong diagnosis. 'I think Abbey is trying to show me that her left lung is higher than her right. I'm being sent a rather weird sensation here, but that's what I'm being told. She's having some trouble breathing so I'd advise you to see a professional. Call your doctor; that's what he's there for.' Luckily I did have some experience of this particular problem through my work with the spirit world. I knew that the feelings I was getting from Abbey were the same as ones I'd dealt with recently from a man who'd had a collapsed lung. I even remembered the technical term for it. 'Abbey's got a pneumothorax,' I exclaimed.

'A what?' asked Abbey's mum.

'One of her lungs isn't as full as the other. It's just like having a collapsed lung. I'm not sure how babies get it but it seems to be what's troubling her.' I was beginning to feel like a doctor. 'Abbey's also telling me that she's not been feeding all that well either. These two problems are linked.'

'I've been noticing that as well. She's been finding it hard to keep her bottle down. Do you know what's causing that?'

'No, Aileen, I don't. I can only tell you what she's trying to tell me. She's only a week old so she's going to tire quickly.'

I left, hoping that Aileen would do something positive. Three months later I got a call asking me to pop over and see her. I was hoping I'd hear good news. Aileen told me the doctor had confirmed that it was common for babies to have one lung higher than the other. He'd diagnosed that Abbey had a floppy larynx – too much skin in her windpipe – which was causing the problem with her breathing. Abbey then told me she was still having difficulty keeping her food down. Aileen explained that Abbey had too much acid in her stomach. She would be having an operation to sort out her problems.

'I'm not sure how much I've helped you then. I've not done much here. I've only managed to confirm things,' I said.

'You've done a great deal, Derek. You gave me the courage to go and see my doctor and kick up a stink about my daughter not getting the help I thought she deserved.'

I'd been living in the cottage for over three years and I still loved it there. Although I was doing theatre shows up and down the country and writing my newspaper columns, money was always tight and I had to be careful with it. I now had a car, just an old Citroën but a total blessing. Physically, I was feeling a great deal stronger. I was slowly recovering mentally from my difficult past but I still wasn't over it. On the odd occasion when I found myself in Glasgow on business I suffered from panic attacks and couldn't get out of the place quickly enough. I knew I had to get my head in order, learn how to relax and not let the past stop me from moving forward.

I recalled my healing session with John, which had really helped me move forward emotionally and spiritually. I called John to see if I could meet with him again but it wasn't possible as situations had changed in his life. He was kind enough, though, to give me the number of his friend, Chris, who lived in Motherwell.

I had some wonderful sessions with Chris. He was a lovely man, very kind and considerate, and when I was with him I felt safe and secure. He did a great deal of healing on me and it felt fabulous. There were a few occasions when I was writhing on the floor and coughing up my demons, as I had previously done with John, but it wasn't as severe as before. I knew that my sensitivity to energy meant I would have to learn to cope with this rather negative side of my work. My sessions with Chris helped me open up more to the spiritual side of my being, and that in turn helped me develop my psychic abilities to an even greater degree. Although I developed considerably through knowing Chris, I felt something was missing. I didn't know what I was really looking for but Chris didn't seem to fulfil all my expectations.

I became rather adept at being able to tell people what was ailing them just by looking at them and concentrating on their body. I started using this technique at theatre shows, which astounded people. I remember being on stage one night and looking at a lady in the front row. I could see from 'looking' at this lady that she had a problem with her right leg. I wasn't sure what that problem was, though I could sense that her left leg seemed to have more energy associated with it than her right. I could feel the imbalance and therefore deduced that her right leg was causing her some difficulty and possibly felt rather stiff. 'I can see that you've been having problems with your right leg, dear,' I said.

'Is that so?' the lady replied. 'What makes you think that?'

'Well, I can see that the energy between your right leg and your left is very different, and this implies that your right leg has been stiff and causing you some problems.'

'Well it has been!' the lady exclaimed. She then bent over in her seat and started to grab and twist her right leg.

'What on earth are you doing?' Inside I began to panic. I didn't want this lady to hurt herself and then try to sue me for damages.

'Don't be daft! I can't hurt myself. My right leg is wooden!' She then grabbed her leg and pulled it free from under her dress, lifting it up for everyone to see. I nearly died! 'Well I was right then.' I exclaimed. 'It is rather stiff!'

A newspaper in Dumbarton ran a story about my ability to communicate with babies. I'll never forget the front page headline: 'Look's who's talking'. There was a photograph of me holding Morgan. The full story was inside, with a classic quote from Aileen: 'I nearly passed out. There is no way Derek could have known the things Morgan was telling him.'

The publicity I'd had in the local press led to the Scottish *Sun* doing a feature on my work. This brought me to the attention of a few television people in London and I was asked to appear on *This Morning* with Phillip Schofield and Fern Britton. I was nervous about going on a live television show and concerned that it would be difficult to communicate with children in a studio environment. I'd noticed that taking any baby or young toddler out of their usual surroundings could sometimes mean they would stop communicating with me.

When I arrived at the studios I felt a sense of foreboding. The production manager asked me to conduct my readings in a tiny, claustrophobic dressing room. This was just about the worst environment in which to try and connect with a baby. I also had to work under very tight time constraints. This was live television and I'd been promised at least half an hour with each baby before we went on air. However, every time I tried to connect or was getting somewhere with one of the babies I would be interrupted by a floor manager or a wardrobe lady or I had to go to make-up. I started to panic, feeling that I'd bitten off more than I could chew.

I was asked to sit on the sofa across from Fern and Philip. Philip put me at ease right away and I really appreciated that. The initial interview went well. I then had five minutes to sit with a pregnant lady in my dressing room and talk to her unborn child. I managed to get a few details from her baby. It wasn't my best reading but it was enough to work with. I was then to connect telepathically with her baby live on the show.

'So Derek, what's the sex of this mum's child?' asked Philip as we went live.

'She's having a boy, Philip.'

'Is that correct?' Philip looked across at the lady and she nodded. Thank God, I thought, at least something is going right! We then went on to talk about some personal details regarding her life and it all fitted in rather well.

The last section of the show was going to be my biggest test. I was to connect with three babies and tell their mums about them. Things went well with the first two babies. There were the usual sore backs and teething problems but some of the information that came through was more than passable. Mum number three, though, seemed to be a total sceptic. She'd been awkward during our few minutes together backstage, and had been more preoccupied with her baby's feed than my reading.

'I'm being told by this baby that she's got a lump on her head,' I said when Philip asked me about her child.

Mum number three wasn't impressed. 'No she's not. I don't know where you got that from!'

'Well, that's what she's telling me.'

'I don't know what you're talking about.' We had run out of time. It wasn't the best way to finish off my feature but I had got through it relatively unscathed. I was upset with mum three, though. The reason? Well, as we walked towards the green room I'm sure I overheard her telling one of the other mums that there was no way she wanted to confirm that her child had a lump on her head in front of three million viewers. I watched her as she rubbed the lump on the back of her daughter's head while she spoke. I learnt a valuable lesson that day: never try to upstage a mum and never do a live show with babies again. Well, not under the constraints I'd agreed with the *This Morning* production team.

Many mums who come to see me are very sceptical but they're willing to suspend their disbelief in the hope that they can help their child. One such mum was Shelley Usher who brought her little boy, Leo, to see me. I found it relatively easy to tune in to Leo. It quickly became apparent that he didn't have too many issues, and that he was a relatively happy soul. Although we didn't meet in his own home he clearly described his house, very early on in his reading. He was very conscious of sending me a picture of what appeared to be a wooden toy he loved to play with. I found myself sitting with pen and paper, drawing precisely the unusual design. It wasn't anything I would have thought an 11-month-old child would play with. I showed it to Shelley.

'Look Shelley. For some strange reason Leo has asked me to draw this wooden structure. There also seems to be something coming through about newspapers and magazines. I'm unsure, though, how this is all connected. There are papers on the floor beside this toy. Leo's been sending me very precise instructions about how it looks. Do you recognize this?' I showed Shelley my drawing.

'Good grief! It's a magazine rack. The one we have in our living room. You've drawn it precisely. It's Leo's favourite thing to play with. In fact, he plays with it so much that he gets into trouble for throwing the newspapers and magazines all over the floor!'

Leo's attention was then redirected and he started to show me a picture in my third eye of a car. He took me to the back seat of this car and then engulfed me with negative feelings. There was anger and frustration in these feelings and I understood exactly what he was trying to say to me.

'Shelley, Leo tells me he doesn't like sitting in the back of the car by himself.'

'Yes, I've noticed how he's been grumbling when he has to sit there on his own. I just put that down to the fact that he seems to be a very sociable little character and likes to be around people.'

'Yes, you've hit the nail on the head there. He is very sociable and he wants you to know how much he misses you when you aren't around.'

'Yes, I miss him when I am working,' said Shelley.

'I'm getting some more information just now from Leo. He's telling me you've been worrying about not being a good enough mum. You seem to think you are not providing Leo with all the things you think he should have in his life. Leo picks up a great deal on your changing emotions and mood swings.'

'Yes, I have been thinking like that recently. That's so true. Normally I'm so good at hiding things,' said Shelley. She started to cry.

'Leo is very aware that you've been feeling vulnerable and he is concerned about you. He wants you to know that he loves you, no matter what.'

'That's amazing because no-one knows how I've been feeling. Not even my husband Vince.'

When the reading was over. Shelley seemed happy. 'I do see Leo in a different light now. I find it incredible that this little soul knows my innermost feelings. Derek, you've convinced me that he was talking to you. Thank you so much.'

I was looking forward to meeting Victoria and her 11-month-old son Sebastian, although I wasn't sure why. As soon as I reached their home in North London I knew that this was going to be a very poignant reading, and it didn't take me long to get to the bottom of it.

'Victoria, I feel very strongly that Sebastian's birth was both a blessing and a negative experience for you,' I said, as I began to tune in to Sebastian's psychic energy. 'Sebastian tells me that before he was born your life was devastated by an emotional trauma. He feels guilty that his birth brought those feelings back to the surface. There is also a strong connection here with a name that's been used before. I guess that Sebastian's trying to tell me that he was named after someone else in the family. Can you help me with that?'

'That's slightly confusing for me. Something did happen to me in the past but I don't understand why Sebastian would mention anything about a name.'

'Sebastian is talking to me at the moment and telling me about another brother. Can his brother walk and talk?'

'Yes, of course he can. His name is Alec and he is seven.'

'No, I'm sorry Victoria. I'm being told about a boy who couldn't walk and couldn't see. There is definitely something coming through from Sebastian about another boy, and it's a brother. I don't think it has anything to do with Alec.'

I then picked up a pen and a piece of paper. Sebastian wanted me to draw how he felt about this brother, the boy who couldn't walk and couldn't see. I took my pen and started to draw two stick men. Sebastian asked me to put a line between each figure to separate them from each other. This was significant. Sebastian was obviously trying to tell me that the bond had been cut between these two boys.

'I'm seeing two boys and then this emotional block, which is horrendous,' I said. 'Do Alec and Sebastian have another brother?'

'I had a 14-month-old son called Lucas,' replied Victoria.

'Can I meet him?'

'He's dead.'

'How did he die?'

'He had a rare brain disorder and hadn't been able to walk or see. We named Sebastian as Sebastian Lucas after his brother.' There was silence. Victoria held her head in her hands. This was a very powerful message and one with significant emotional connotations.

'Sebastian tells me that he gets very distressed when you think about or talk about Lucas,' I said. 'Sebastian senses that he was sent to heal you and your family. He feels awful, knowing that his birth brought lots of deeply held grief to the surface for you.'

It had been an astounding reading and one I wouldn't forget in a hurry. Victoria had been very tearful and emotional, so we had a coffee in the kitchen while she calmed down. I asked her what she thought about the reading. 'The greatest lesson I've taken from this, Derek, is that I must try to move on with my life and not dwell on the traumas of the past, for Sebastian's sake as well as my own. You've been able to pick up on the most poignant things from both my past and my present, as well as everyday details. It's been an amazing experience and I want to thank you so much for coming.'

Spreading the word

I've come to the conclusion that a baby transmits waves of energy, in much the same way as a spirit. When I become attuned to these energy waves I receive the information, rather like a radio picking up the sounds sent out by the transmitter at a radio station. These pictures and feelings can be instant and clear but the information can also be slow, unfocused and confusing.

Every baby communicates on a different wavelength and vibrates at a different frequency. It's just like a tele-pathic fingerprint. I've noticed that twins vibrate at similar frequencies, though the vibrations are dissimilar enough for me to be able to tell them apart.

I met with 20-month-old twins Joe and Georgina in London with their mum Laura. Within the first few seconds of meeting Joe and Georgina I could sense that the reading wasn't going to go as well as I'd hoped. Although Joe seemed fairly receptive, Georgina didn't suffer fools gladly and told me in no uncertain terms that she wasn't going to communicate with me. Well, at least not directly.

So Georgina went to play upstairs and I began with Joe, but only on his terms. Laura seemed curious about my abilities but a little sceptical too. I noticed that she was nervous and slightly perplexed by me. I concluded that maybe she was afraid that I could actually do what I said I could, and that she might find it difficult to comprehend the implications.

Joe played continually and we had absolutely no eye contact. He seemed very protective of his sister. They had made it clear to me from the first moment we met that they were very proud of their bond and no-one was going to come between them. They also didn't want me to share in what they thought was their own unique way of communicating with each other. They seemed to be slightly taken aback by me. Here was someone who could talk to them on their level, the level they obviously thought no-one else could tune in to.

'I realize that Georgina is upstairs at the moment with your mum, Laura, but she has a special bond with Joe so he's going to do all her talking for her. Is that okay with you?' I asked Laura.

'No problem at all.'

'This reading may be over before it starts though. I'm not feeling too confident. I get the impression that neither of your twins really wants to communicate with me today. It's a pity but let's see how it goes. Joe and Georgina can talk to each other telepathically and I'm going to try and listen in to their conversations, Laura.'

Laura seemed impressed. It was time, though, to say something that would shock her.

'Joe is telling me about his favourite toy. Is it here?'

'No, it's not.'

'I can hear sirens, and keep being shown a flashing light.'

'Yes, his favourite toy is a toy phone, which plays countless loud noises and has a flashing light. It's not in this room. That's impressive.'

I could feel the constant background noise of Joe and Georgina talking to each other as I sat there, totally frustrated. It was infuriating. It was as if they had some coding device and could lock me out of their conversations. I could just about make out the odd word and phrase, though, so it wasn't all bad. I started to tell Laura family details and information about her life. The twins didn't like it when I didn't talk about them so Georgina butted in with a little piece of information.

'Georgina just said that she likes to twist and turn the silver disc on your hand or wrist.'

Laura seemed impressed. 'Yes, she does that with my engagement ring.'

Then Joe came up with some stuff of his own. 'Joe tells me you've got another son who seems to have some difficulty holding his knife and fork. He has quite a few foibles.'

'That's correct,' said Laura. I saw that she was starting to warm to me.

'You know Laura, Joe tells me that you'll need to get your car windscreen repaired. It seems to have a crack in it. I'm also being told that you slipped on some paving slabs and hurt your foot last week.'

'Yes, that's right. I need a new windscreen and I hurt my foot when I was outside. It's amazing how you knew that.'

'Joe keeps showing me a picture in my third eye of a silver vessel. He wants to play with it but for some reason you will not let him. He seems frustrated that you are being so particular about not letting him get his hands on it.' I picked up a pen and paper and drew that vessel for Laura.

Laura was quick to answer. 'Yesterday I put some tulips in a silver vase and set them on a high window ledge. Joe wanted to get his hands on it but it was well out of his reach.'

It was all over. The communication link just stopped and I was left high and dry. 'Sorry Laura. This has been a difficult reading for me. Your twins just weren't in the mood to talk all that much to me today.'

'I've really enjoyed it though,' said Laura. 'I've definitely got a better understanding of the twins and how they are feeling. My cynicism melted away within the first 20 minutes of the reading.' I was happy to hear that!

Over the years there have been countless surprises in the messages I get from babies. I'm constantly telling mums and dads that it's not me who's 'amazing'; it's their child for being able to send me the message. As no two readings are alike, I'm filled with as much anticipation before each reading as the parents probably are.

A child's personality shines through when I communicate telepathically with them. If the child is of a quiet or emotional disposition or a bit of a loner then the reading will be exactly like that: sensitive, assured and probably intense. If, though, the child is brash, loud and outgoing then the reading will be fast and furious and probably over in 10 minutes! I was looking forward to meeting pregnant mum Julika Schulz. Julika's baby wasn't due for two months and she was really interested in finding out more about it. She seemed keen to know what it was thinking and what sort of personality it had.

Julika worked as a director for a German television network. She wanted to film our meeting so that it could be shown on German television. I was slightly nervous about recording our session, just in case something came through that was too personal to be shown to millions of viewers. Julika reassured me, though, that she would be editing the proceedings. I told Julika that I didn't have much experience of talking to babies who were still in the womb, but we were both willing to give it a try.

I sat beside Julika on her sofa and placed my hand a few inches from her tummy. I started to get myself tuned in, and once I could feel some images coming through I knew that I was in the zone. 'The first thing I'm being shown could be sensitive. Are you sure I can continue the reading with the cameras rolling?'

'That's no problem.'

'Okay, well your baby tells me that you and his father are not married.'

'Yes, that's correct.'

'Your baby keeps showing me a building site. I can see work being done on a house and there seems to be problems with light fittings. There are paint tins all over the floor.' The images were fairly strong but occasionally blurred into each other so I found it difficult to be precise.

'Yes, my boyfriend David and I are trying to move into our new flat but we've been having countless problems with the work and it seems to have been dragging on for ages now.'

'When you mentioned David just now, your baby told me that he has a mark on his face. It's not a permanent mark but it's noticeable. You've obviously both been talking about it.'

'David's got a cold sore on his lip.'

'Yes, and I've just been told to tell you that your baby knows about the fungus he has on his toe!'

'That's amazing! How could my baby know that?'

'Well, you've been talking with David haven't you? Your baby's been listening in to the conversation. That's pretty obvious isn't it?'

Julika seemed slightly perturbed by my statement. I guess she was beginning to realize that her private conversations with her boyfriend weren't so private after all! We then went on to talk about relationships. 'Your baby is showing me a man and woman going through some sort of relationship turmoil. They seem to be always at each other's throats. There is a great deal of arguing taking place in these images and your baby is upset by them. Have you and David had a fallout, Julika?'

'No, we don't argue like that.'

'Look, I don't want to call you a liar. We could turn the cameras off if you want? I don't want to cause offence.'

'No, there is no need. I've no idea what messages you are getting through here.'

'Maybe we should think this through and take it easy. I'm being shown a man and a woman arguing. Perhaps the images aren't of you and David.'

Julika thought for a moment. 'I get it! David is having problems with his ex-wife at the moment and they are going through a divorce. Things haven't been easy for David recently because of that.'

'Yes, your baby's just confirmed that to me. Now I'm being shown a number of images here, Julika, and we need to work through this message. I'm also getting a pain in my chest, which also seems significant.' I felt I had to take a moment to try and work out what I was being shown by this baby. 'The first thing I want to say is that I'm being directed to look at your breast, Julika. I realize this may sound weird to you but that's what your baby wants me to do.'

'That's okay.'

'I'm also getting a tight pain across my own chest. I've never felt anything like this before. It's nothing that would indicate that your child is trying to tell me about a medical problem. When I connect with children they seem to know which technique to use to show me about heart attacks or lumps. I'm slightly baffled.'

'Can you tell me some more? Maybe I can help you.'

'Well, I'm being shown two other images but they don't seem connected in any way. I'm being told to tell you about, of all things, bras! The other image is of a shop front. Maybe your baby is giving me a pain across my chest in order to tell me to wear a bra!'

Julika looked astounded. Had I crossed the line with her? Did she think I was some sort of pervert? I hoped not. 'That's amazing. I was talking to my mum on the phone the other day. My mum owns a bra shop in a village in northern Germany!' I was stunned. 'We were discussing her shop when she called. My baby must have heard what we were talking about.'

I was over the moon. What an amazing message to come through in a reading, especially from a baby who was still in the womb! I did get one thing glaringly wrong, though. After the cameras had been put away I told Julika that I thought she was going to have a boy. Two months after her reading she gave birth to Nikolina, a beautiful baby girl! I can't be right all the time I suppose!

A few days later I received a message from Tom McShane who lived in Cumbernauld. Tom said in his message that his wife had just passed away and that her spirit had come through to talk to me during a private reading I'd just given to his sister-in-law. Tom was desperate to hear from his wife and was therefore calling to arrange a private reading for himself.

I was pleasantly surprised when I met with Tom. For some reason we just clicked. His wife's spirit was astoundingly strong and the reading turned out to be one of the best I'd ever done. I was actually taken aback by my accuracy, which is saying something because I'm normally my own worst critic.

During the reading it became clear to me that Tom was a very spiritual man. As well as being a Reiki healer, he had also studied Zen. From that moment I knew Tom was going to be my new guide and would help me to deal with my demons. He would help me move forward in my life and to grow both spiritually and psychically. The energy around him and his home was astonishing and I wanted more of it.

Deborah Welsh was keen to meet with me because she was going through some major changes in her life and wanted to know if her son, Robbie, had picked up on any of her trials and tribulations. I met with Deborah and Robbie in their home in Larkhall, Lanarkshire. When I connected with 10-month-old Robbie, Deborah was taken aback by the personal details I mentioned. She was stunned to hear that Robbie had picked up on rows over his name while he was still in the womb. 'Robbie tells me that you wanted to call him Jamie,' I said.

'Yes, that's true but how would he know that? I was still pregnant at the time.'

'Well, this is his way of validating that he is actually communicating with me.'

'We were going to call him after his grandfather.'

'I don't want to get heavy,' I said, 'but Robbie's concerned about you. He tells me that he's a bit of a mummy's boy and is very close to you. Have you wondered why he's been so clingy recently?' Deborah seemed surprised. 'You've been having a few issues at work, haven't you? There's someone bothering you who sits to the right of your desk. Robbie tells me it's got so bad that you are thinking of leaving.'

'Yes, that's very true. It's astounding what he's telling you. I try not to bring my work home with me but I must be if he's picking up on it.'

'Well, you are bringing your work home with you and these tensions are affecting Robbie too, you know.'

'That upsets me.'

'He's telling me that you have also been considering moving house. This is unsettling him too. He's a scared little boy at the moment. Not all children enjoy sudden change in their life.'

'I'd hate to think that he feels insecure. I love him and only want the best for him.'

'Yes, I can see that but you need to be careful. He's getting mixed messages, you know. What you say to him is not necessarily what you are thinking deep inside.

Children aren't stupid. They know when you are bullshitting them.'

'That makes sense. I suppose you are right. I never thought of it like that before. I'll start to tell to him what's going on in my life and explain more about how I feel.'

'Don't lay it on thick, though. He is still a baby, but don't lie to him either. He'll know when you are fibbing anyway, and he'll soon let you know about it.'

I travelled over to Paisley to see a baby and her mum. I first met Sarah White when her daughter Naomi was just three months old. I'd been asked to make a return visit now Naomi was one.

Naomi had been having tantrums and Sarah was worried. She'd taken Naomi to the doctor but he couldn't help, and her childminder had said that if Naomi's behaviour didn't improve then she wouldn't be able to look after her any more. I wasn't worried, though, because I knew from the meeting I'd had with Naomi nine months previously that she was very easy to communicate with. Sure enough, it wasn't long before I'd hit on exactly what was troubling her. 'I can pinpoint this issue very quickly. You left Naomi with a friend who didn't change her wet nappy, didn't you?'

'Yes, I did, but that was five months ago.'

'Well, that's the whole cause of your problem. Naomi is telling me that she is confused and hurt about that. This friend seems to have a poor reputation with you now. Am I correct?'

'I suppose I have a great deal of anger regarding the way Naomi was treated.' Sarah's face reddened. She was starting to get upset.

'Well, your anger is rubbing off on Naomi. She's also upset about what happened to her and the only way she can deal with that is to have a tantrum. She's now scared about being left alone without you.'

'Well, I have noticed that when I leave her she starts to play up.'

'Naomi tells me that she feels trapped in her playpen and hates being shut in behind any closed door.'

'Yes, I can understand that.'

'Exactly, and I bet that when your mum or close family members come round you are constantly talking about your own problems. How do you think Naomi copes with that? It's confusing her. Try to stop talking openly about your financial worries. They are also upsetting Naomi.'

'I've been trying to work things out recently. I'd no idea that this could upset my daughter.' Sarah was obviously distressed.

'Now, she's also telling me that she's confused about the way she should act towards her dad. She thinks that if she shows him any love then she's going against you. It's a terrible position for a baby to be in. I'm sorry to say this but you are the root cause of the problem.'

'I feel awful.'

'I just feel that I've let my baby down.'

'You've not let her down. You've made a couple of mistakes but that doesn't mean you can't solve your issues with her dad. Maybe you need to stand back from this and start to realize that your ex-partner is still the father of your child and has a right to be respected for that.'

'I'll try but I can't promise anything. I'm not perfect.'

'No-one said you had to be perfect. Just be Naomi's mum, not the mother of your ex-partner's child.'

By this stage I wanted to move away from my medium work and become known as a baby mind reader. I still wanted to do theatre shows and private readings but I didn't want the public to get confused about me or, worse still, be scared to ask me to see their child because I was associated with the dead.

I travelled quite a distance to meet with Hazel Stirling and her eight-month-old baby boy, Aidan. Aidan's dad, Lee, was in the room when I arrived and I quickly asked him to leave. I knew from his body language and the energy around him that he would get in the way of the reading. I needed all my concentration to connect with Aidan.

The first image I received from Aidan was rather standard stuff. 'Aidan keeps showing me a pram. He was unhappy with that pram and it scared him. I get the impression that it was rather rickety and had a wobbly wheel. I'm certain he's trying to tell me it wasn't new when you bought it.'

'Before Aidan was born we got him a second-hand pram. It's on the scrapheap now,' Hazel replied. She seemed perplexed.

'He likes his new one,' I added. Hazel relaxed. 'I don't want to appear rude,' I continued, 'but Aidan tells me that you were pregnant out of wedlock.'

'Yes. That's spot on.'

'I gather from Aidan that his dad smokes. Lee should give it up. Even though he never does this in front of Aidan, it seems to be important that he stops.'

'I'm sure that'll be an incentive for Lee to give up.'

'Aidan's pleased that you've now put his bracelet in a safer place.'

'How on earth did you know that?' exclaimed Hazel.

'Well, he just told me that it had been lying around for a while. It's in the right-hand side of the drawer upstairs. What's the hospital connection with the bracelet?'

'It's the one he had on when he was in the maternity ward.'

'Can I get personal?'

'Yes, of course you can.'

'You had a lump on your breast, didn't you?'

'Yes, I did. That was a while ago. I've no idea how Aidan would know that.'

'Well, you worried about that lump, even though it wasn't anything too serious.'

'Like every woman I was concerned.'

'It's a memory you still carry around with you. It's in your subconscious and Aidan can pick up on that. Maybe now is the time to let those thoughts go. These chains are stopping you from moving forward with your life.'

'Yes, I suppose they are, but sometimes it's difficult to let go of the past.'

'I can understand that but we have to think about the implications for your child. I need to validate this further for you,' I said. 'I don't want you to think I'm making this advice up. It's coming through from Aidan so I'll tell you something that is totally spot on.'

'Okay, but don't scare me. This has been traumatic enough.'

'Well, Aidan knows about your mum having a miscarriage a few years ago. He tells me that she lost a boy. This boy, Aidan's uncle, is here with us at this very moment and watches over Aidan.'

'I'm gobsmacked. No-one knows about that apart from close family. I'm amazed at what you've just told me. I'm delighted too that Aidan has spoken to me but it's all a bit weird and difficult to take in.'

'I understand that but it's precious, so don't forget about today. Look at the benefits you've both got out of this reading and move on from there.'

I started to see Tom McShane on a regular basis after our first meeting. These visits were a revelation to me. I would sit with Tom and he'd explain clearly and concisely how I should deal with the problems I thought I had, and he would advise me on how I could grow spiritually and psychically. He talked about the ego and how we develop it to such an extent that it engulfs us and controls our lives. I knew exactly what he was talking about as I realized that this is what had happened to me during my dark days. He tried to explain about completeness, forgiveness and compassion – those things that come from within. Each meeting had its own unique, amazing experience and provided me with the balance I needed. Tom had become my mentor.

Tom was also a healer and I would regularly arrange sessions. I was working very hard at this time, flying around the UK doing various features for radio stations, magazines and newspapers as well as private readings. Because of my sensitivity to energy, I was picking up a great deal of negative energy on my travels. I was still writhing and vomiting during these healing sessions, but after each cleansing I noticed that less and less negative energy was clinging on to my body. Maybe I was beginning to protect myself by staying positive and focused.

I began to see Tom at least twice a week. I wanted to grow both as a human being and a spiritual being. I could feel myself changing, becoming less stressed and anxious and more relaxed and content. My readings developed too, and I began to help more children through my work as a baby mind reader, and more people who wanted to connect with those they'd lost to the spirit world. It wasn't always easy, though, and I still had down days, but I didn't let these thoughts take over as much as I used to.

I was approached a few years ago by *Closer* magazine. I was asked to meet with associate editor Louise Oswald and her six-month-old son, Max. Then I was to pop over and see Beverly Turner – the television presenter, author and wife of Olympic gold medallist James Cracknell – and talk to her baby boy, Croyde, who was 11 months old. After all that, I was to pay a visit to former Page Three model and Living TV presenter, Melinda Messenger, and her eight-month-old daughter, Evie. It was going to be a very busy day.

When I arrived at Louise's London home, I focused and got straight into my zone. I took one look at Max and we seemed to connect. Immediately, he told me that his dad, Brian, had a sore tooth. I felt this was a good start, especially as no-one apart from Brian knew anything about his toothache. I could sense there was also a story coming through about Max not liking some new black-out curtains Louise had just bought. Louise confirmed that she'd spent a fortune on those curtains which still, to her annoyance, 'let the light in'. Max went from one extreme to the other, and the reading became rather mundane very quickly. It seemed to me that everyone thought I was wasting their time. I needed good strong validations, but it wasn't that easy to get any juicy information from Max.

There were a couple of things that shocked Louise. I mentioned about Max liking a bracelet his mum wore, which had been discarded in the lounge. I also got a strong image from Max about some new blue shoes he wanted to wear. There were a few other non-specific things but that was about it. Louise didn't say much but was surprised when she started to rummage through her lounge and found the bracelet she'd lost. She also told me that an old friend had bought Max a pair of blue D&G trainers, which he had seen for only a few seconds before they'd been packed away for future use, and there was 'no way I could have known that'. I was disappointed with the reading but Louise told me that I'd given her some real clues about Max and how he felt about things. I knew I'd really need to hit some targets if I was going to get a good piece in the magazine.

I met with Beverly Turner and her little boy Croyde in their flat in London. From the minute I got there I knew it was going to be an utter waste of everyone's time. Croyde just didn't want to talk to me and that was it. I tried – my God, I tried – but whenever I attempted to connect with him he blocked me. He seemed happy enough when I was there though. He wasn't moody and never had a tantrum. He just played on the floor like a normal happy soul and wandered around Beverly's lounge, totally ignoring me. No matter what I did, he just would not communicate with me on any level whatsoever. I looked at Beverly and she looked at me and I shrugged my shoulders. I had to admit defeat within the first few minutes. I'd been scheduled to stay for an hour and it was torment.

Melinda's daughter was slightly easier to talk to. I did manage to connect with Evie but it was difficult to tune in and keep the communication channels open. She did tell me a few things but it was all fairly standard stuff, I'm afraid to say. Evie seemed to be concerned about her new bedroom, which Melinda confirmed was correct. She seemed impressed when I commented that Evie had told me that her bedroom was next to the bathroom, or that she had an en-suite bathroom. Evie also mentioned that she'd been shopping with Melinda for a 'pretty party dress with a frill around the bottom' and that 'someone in the family had a bad leg', but apart from a few other bits and pieces that was really it. Melinda was a joy to be with, though, and I loved spending time with her. She was so kind and was very open and honest with me. She explained that Wayne, her husband, had just had an operation on his leg after suffering a football injury, and that I was absolutely spot on about the dress.

I was disappointed though. I'd been with children who could tell me so much more. Maybe I'd put needless pressure on myself because I felt I needed this to work, but for me the information just wasn't coming through. It had been a difficult day but it's one I'll always remember, even if the mums and their babies don't! It helped to shape my career forever so I honestly can't thank the people at *Closer* enough.

I decided on the way back from Melinda's home that I would only meet with children who had problems and issues, those who had sleeping, eating or behavioural problems. Children who have issues normally have a lot more to say than children who don't. I didn't want to waste my time or anyone else's — no matter how famous their mums were — providing a bit of titillation.

Understanding my gift – how I communicate with babies

I'm very grateful for my gift and I'd never take it for granted, but I don't believe I'm the only person with this talent. It may sound strange but I believe we are all born psychic. Somehow I've managed to tune in to this phenomenon, not by some quirk of fate or act of God, but through opening up to the signals that children give out.

No-one would question the talent of David Beckham. As a boy he had raw talent but he has trained a great deal and worked hard on his skills throughout his career. He's realized that in order to keep on top of his game he has to stay focused. I can also kick a ball but I have nowhere near the talent of Mr Beckham. I'm certain, however, that if I spent a few hours with him on a football pitch I would become a better player, even in that short time. David would I'm sure impart a great deal of his knowledge to me and give me the benefit of his years of football experience.

In the same way, I believe that my skills can be taught to others, if they are willing to listen and learn.

I believe the reason I can communicate with babies is because I have developed my psychic abilities and the spiritual side of my being. Maybe my time living alone has helped me. Many other people could communicate fully with their children if they reached a level where they were ready to allow that psychic skill into their life.

Not all babies are psychic. Those who are, though, communicate on two levels. They send pictures to my third eye, which is situated just above and between the eyes; this is known as 'clairvoyance'. They also send me feelings, such as hurt and anguish, which are felt in the solar plexus; this is 'clairsentience'. Sometimes they send me pain to communicate that certain parts of their body are sore or to give me further details about a message.

Clairvoyance and clairsentience are very different techniques but I have learnt to use them both to my advantage when I communicate with children telepathically. For instance, I may not fully understand a particular message initially because it's been shown to me through only one means, say clairvoyance. Once, though, the child understands my difficulty, they may send me a second message by clairsentience in order for me to get a complete understanding of the information. By focusing my mind on particular feelings and important events I can also transmit images and emotions back to children.

Throughout my career as a baby mind reader I've followed certain clear steps in order to prepare and get myself into the zone. The zone is what I call the area in my mind where I go to connect telepathically with babies and young children. I have to concentrate fully on this particular place in order to receive and transmit messages.

It's not that difficult for anyone to find their own zone. It may just take a little time. Your zone is like your own private telephone exchange. It's the place where I go in order to receive and make calls. If I don't go there to communicate with a child then it's like leaving my phone off the hook. I'll never get any messages!

Here is an exercise you could try to help you find your zone. For this to work it's imperative that you are relaxed, preferably sitting upright in your favourite armchair.

You are consciously reading this book at the moment. Have you noticed, though, how you are reacting to it? Stop reading and think about your level of focus. Concentrate on this focus or dream state for a minute and where thoughts are materializing in your head. Try to remember this location. In time and through practice you'll be able to go to this place very quickly. Then, try to concentrate on how you adapt to other, everyday thoughts popping into your head when you are doing such things as reading a book or thinking about a memory. Try to capture the point in your brain where these thoughts come to you. They should always materialize at the same place. I normally get these images above my right eye, on my temple. Therefore, I know that's where I need to go when I want to communicate with a child. You'll find your spot, although it may take some time. Try to practise by 'jumping' in and out from one thought to another; focus on a daydream when you are in the middle of a chore or task. By doing this you'll be able to define the difference between your 'zone' and your 'normal' everyday frame of reference more easily.

In order to communicate with a baby I have to connect with the unconscious areas of the mind. One way in which I do this is through stillness. Some call it meditation. When moments of relative quiet arise in your life you become more aware of the highly desirable energy that flows from this peace. This positive energy helps you grow psychically and develop the ability required to connect with a child on that level. This energy change also helps to weaken the negative machinery that's been holding you back. It enables you to look at your daily routine from a different, more positive perspective.

Our lives are full of noise. The most important noise we have to deal with, though, is mind noise, that endless stream of involuntary thoughts – much of which is the same old stuff going round in circles. When you focus on a specific task and give it your full attention, you will find that the amount of mind noise will be reduced dramatically, perhaps to the point of non-existence. This state of mind is often achieved by top sportspeople, artists or musicians, and allows the full flow of creativity.

To achieve this you need to get away from the unconscious habit of filling every second of your life with thought. Becoming more aware of what is actually going on in your head is the first step in reducing your mind noise. By doing this you activate a part of you that's been lying dormant. This will ultimately help you to develop your psychic skills and your ability to communicate telepathically.

I now spend more time observing, rather than filling my life with the constant distractions offered by television, radio and such like. Apart from my normal pursuits and practical daily routine, I have made this my goal. I have to do this if I want to be free of mind noise.

Daydreaming is another good way to open up to our true selves. Letting your mind wander without thought and prejudice helps you enter areas of your mind that your conscious self has never allowed you to visit before.

As with any journey, the more I have travelled along these paths, the easier that journey has become. Within a short time and through a little practice I was able to visit these unconscious areas of my mind quickly, and found it easier to accept the messages sent to me by children.

It's very easy to get involved in other people's dramas, especially where children are concerned. It may seem harsh but in order to place myself in the zone and connect on a telepathic level I've had to learn to distance myself emotionally from any child's personal trauma. If I don't then the negative energy set off by these dramas will really affect my ability to connect with them.

By developing some of the above methods I soon found that I could receive sophisticated messages from a child who hadn't even developed language. I communicate with the higher centres of a child, parts they are not fully conscious of, but at a point where a level of consciousness exists.

No-one said this was going to be easy – far from it. It takes practice and perseverance. The most important thing I've learnt is to pace myself, to take one step at a time. I've also told myself that I'll never be able to run a marathon if I'm finding it difficult to walk down to the local shops!

Being able to communicate with a child on a telepathic level is fundamentally about energy. On average, we use only about eight per cent of our brain capacity. We have enough electrical energy in our brains to start a car. If we produce electricity then we must therefore produce magnetic fields, and this implies that we must be sending out electrical impulses from our brains that can be monitored. Telepathy is about tuning in to those signals and that energy.

We have seven energy points on our body. These chakras were identified by Eastern mystics thousands of years ago. The third eye chakra is located in the centre of our forehead. A blockage there may cause headaches. The solar plexus chakra is where we get our gut feelings from and is very sensitive. Unsettled stomachs are a sure sign of imbalance and discord in our lives. We use our third eye and solar plexus chakras to communicate with babies and young children.

To be able to connect psychically, I firstly deal with any serious blockages I may have around my chakras, particularly in my third eye and solar plexus. It's fundamental that I cleanse myself of the negative energy that I have built up within and around myself during my day and over the past weeks, months and years. This process allows lucidity and clarity, and enables a shift in consciousness to occur.

I find a quiet space that's free from clutter. While doing this I try to relax and free my mind from tension and the stresses and strains of the day. The more positive I feel and the more open I am to this routine, the more successful it is for me.

I begin by standing upright in the middle of my chosen space and breathing deeply. I try to focus solely on my breathing, allowing all my troubles to float away with each outward breath. It's very important during this time that I constantly try to clear my mind of negative thoughts. I've learnt to detach myself from any particular worries I may have, no matter how difficult that may be. I try to think of nothing, but thoughts do inevitably pop up so I endeavour to let them go as soon as they appear. The clearer I am the more focused I'll be. The only thing I'm aware of is my breathing.

I've realized that it's important to work upwards through my body, cleansing it and pushing away any negative feelings. I expel the energy built up during this task through my mouth so I keep my mouth opened slightly during these cleansing sessions. I've noticed that as I work through each chakra area I begin to feel more alive and less imbalanced, negative or depressed. My fears and worries become manageable and less scary. I keep concentrating on those parts of the body where I feel the most stress and strain. If I need more time in a specific area then I take it.

When we communicate with each other verbally, we use many of our senses to recognize and interpret the information being sent to us. We notice the body language of those we are in conversation with; we listen to the words spoken and their inflection. We sense the way in which the story is being conveyed to us, the intensity of the conversation and the mood and feelings of the language.

When I connect with a child telepathically, using my sixth sense, many of these everyday communication techniques are not available to me. The child is then in total control of that connection. The conversation is always based upon the child's need to communicate and what they want to talk about.

When a psychic connection is made, there can be a strong urge on my part to get straight to the point of concern, such as why the child keeps crying or having tantrums. Many parents contact me because their babies are having trouble sleeping. The parents may not have had a full night's sleep for months. In these cases, I always hope that the child will quickly reveal what the difficulty is. Thankfully, in 99 per cent of cases the reasons do come out in the end, even if parents have to be patient. Sometimes I have to take things slowly as my way of conversing with a child may appear as strange or unusual to them as it does to me.

I remember doing a reading for parents Amanda and Matt and their six-month-old son, Andrew. I arrived at their home just after Andrew had been fed. Andrew seemed tired and instantly fell asleep. This didn't concern me as I knew I could communicate with sleeping children.

Matt made some coffee and Amanda began to tell me what their problem was. 'Andrew just will not sleep at night. It's been really difficult.'

I started to tune in to Andrew and immediately began to get a pain in my back. 'Something's been bothering Andrew and it's affecting his back,' I said. I went back to Andrew and asked what was troubling him. 'He seems to have an extra sheet in his bed which is causing him some discomfort at the moment. He's telling me that it's under his back and it's stopping him from getting any sleep. He can't work out why it stops halfway down his back. That's one of the reasons why he's keeping you up all night.'

'We've recently put a waterproof sheet in his cot,' said Matt.

'Well, it's time to reconsider that. Andrew also doesn't like it when you close the door on him when he's in his bedroom. If you keep the door open and ditch the water-proof sheet then you'll be sleeping like a log tonight!' Everyone in the room looked sceptical. It was obviously time to say something dramatic. I went back to Andrew and connected with him. By this time it was much easier to tune in.

'Well, well, so you two have been arguing then?' I looked at Matt and Amanda and both of their faces went bright red. 'Andrew tells me that one of you threw a cup at the other and it's made a mark on the hallway wall.'

Matt's face was scarlet. 'Amanda threw it at me!' he exclaimed. He seemed suddenly convinced of my talents. Amanda still looked puzzled. I connected with Andrew again and asked him if he would tell me something about his mum. Kindly, he obliged. 'Andrew tells me you've been in hospital, Amanda. I'm being told this was to do with a blood test?'

'Yes, that's correct.'

'Well, Andrew's just told me that they couldn't get blood out of one of your arms and they had to use the other one instead.'

'My God, that's totally true.' Amanda now seemed more convinced but there was more to come.

'Andrew is showing me three things. The first is polished shoes, the second is a card or a photograph and the third is about an older gentleman. I'm unsure of the connection though. That part Andrew is not telling me.'

'My dad stayed over last night. Could he be the older gentleman?' asked Amanda.

'Possibly, but we need it all to fit. Would it help if I said that when I'm shown polished shoes by a baby it's usually to signify a policeman or someone who works in the services?'

'Well, what if I were to tell you that the reason my dad stayed over last night was because he's going to work for the military in the Falklands and he had to go to Edinburgh today to get his ID card made!'

I heard from Amanda a few days later. 'Derek, Andrew's been great. We are finally getting some much needed kip. I was always very sceptical about psychics and thought they preyed on the weak-minded but I'm so impressed by you.'

Children send me pictures and feelings in various forms. Some are easy to understand but most are cryptic and rather confusing. One baby's interpretation of an event can be totally different from another's. A baby's likes and dislikes will also become apparent when they send me messages. Those things they enjoy will be more noticeable and prevalent. Messages can also be conveyed to me in a form that a baby easily recognizes but I do not. Young children don't necessarily build a picture of their state of mind from the foundations up. They sometimes work from the roof down, so at times it can be hard to interpret what is being said.

Messages are always sent from the baby's perspective. That's how it works. I've had to learn to put myself in the baby's shoes before beginning to interpret the messages I'm given. The information being sent to me may not be what I assume it is, and a picture can tell many stories. I find it easier to work out exactly what the messages mean if I build up a bond with the child during the reading.

If I get stuck on something then I let the child know by telling them verbally. Simple phrases like, 'I don't know what that means' or 'Can you show me that picture again please?' really help. Saying out loud what I think the child is trying to say also helps them realize that they are being fully and easily understood. When these situations occur a child will then move on to the next piece of information they deem important.

I always have to remember that these telepathic conversations may not follow logical patterns, and the time spent connecting in this way with a child, although enlightening, is sometimes energy-sapping. It's difficult, but I try not to take the blame. If I'm having a bad day and finding it difficult to connect or understand the meaning in things, I console myself with the thought that the child may be tired, not in the mood or simply not interested. The child may not be happy with their surroundings, or may not want to spill the beans on the various issues within their family!

I recall one reading with a baby boy called Jackson. His mum, Jane Brocklebank, had asked me to visit. I got the impression that she just wanted to check me out. Before we met, Jane told me that Jackson was four months old and had an older sister called Jess who was three, but other than that I knew nothing about the family. I had focused myself before travelling over to see Jackson, and I remember feeling very positive when I arrived.

Initially, Jackson was fairly easy to tune in to, although there were a couple of things I couldn't quite understand. I soon worked out that he couldn't get his head around the fact that he could 'talk' to me. I explained this to Jane but we decided to continue with the reading.

During the first few minutes of the reading, Jackson kept showing me a picture of a tower with an aerial on the top. Jane didn't seem to understand what this could mean so we sat for a while contemplating the image. Had Jackson been looking at a book or noticed this building during a family holiday? There were so many possibilities that I felt we were going nowhere, that is until Jackson began to talk to me about bedrooms. Within a few sentences I had accurately described both Jane and Jackson's bedrooms, and this in turn helped Jane understand what Jackson was trying to tell us. 'There is a statue of the Chrysler Building in our bedroom,' said a rather flustered Jane, 'and there is also a picture of the

Flatiron Building in New York!' She seemed amazed and so was I.

Within the 10 or so minutes of meeting Jackson, I could see he was beginning to understand that to be fully coherent he had to send me multiple images that would help me build up a story in my mind of what he was trying to convey to me. Only then could I fathom out what he was trying to say. Thankfully, there was more to come.

I realized that we both needed Jane to stay as alert as possible so that she could help me to understand fully what Jackson wanted to talk to her about. Throughout the reading, Jackson kept telling me about two dates that seemed really important to him. I felt that this was unsettling Jackson, and that he was anxious for his mum to understand what he was trying to say. 'I'm being shown two dates, Jane,' I said. 'One is a party or anniversary and the other, Jackson tells me, "was made for him".' I looked at Jane and saw that this had struck a chord.

'Jackson was born by elective Caesarean three weeks before his sister's birthday.' At last, we were getting somewhere. I just needed Jane to stay focused and we'd be okay.

'There seems to be a great deal coming through from Jackson about an older chap who has a heart problem,' I said. 'This chap has funny feet and gardens are important to him. I can also make something out about, of all things, a television remote control. It seems to be broken. These issues are all connected and you should know about them.'

Jane looked at me and smiled. 'That's my dad!' she exclaimed. 'That's phenomenal!' I had struck another chord. 'Dad's got angina and his feet turn upwards. Dad's remote control is broken and he loves cutting the grass and being in his garden.'

I had another question for Jane. 'Were the paving stones laid properly?'

Jane looked at me again and smiled. 'That's our paving stones. They've been lifted up and replaced recently and the surface was wobbly. It really bugged me.'

I was pleased that Jane now felt I was actually connecting with Jackson but there were a couple of things I still needed to say. 'Jackson tells me that your dad has had a muscular problem around his shoulder.'

'Well, I know nothing about that, unless Jackson has some insider knowledge.' Jane seemed disappointed that I'd seemingly not hit the mark but I wasn't surprised. Older people have a tendency to keep some things close to their chest, especially when it's connected to their health and they don't want to worry their family.

There was one last thing Jackson mentioned to me but Jane was unable to confirm it. He told me that he had some food allergies, but as Jane was still breast-feeding she said she didn't know of any. At the end of the reading Jane seemed convinced. Things had gone quite well. Considering Jackson was only four months old he had quite a lot to say for himself.

Sometimes the messages transmitted to us from our children lose their clarity en route or seem to get tangled up with other messages. I often find it helpful to actually draw these images. It's also possible that a number of images are connected to one event, not separate stories. A child may also transmit images to me and I'll have absolutely no idea what they mean because I'm not 'in the know'. If this happens during a reading I allow the mum to do all the talking, especially if the child refuses to help me by elaborating on a particular message.

I once sat with a mum, Anna, and her 11-month-old daughter, Eloise, for just a few minutes, and the amount of different information that came through was amazing. Initially, this reading hadn't gone that well as I seemed to be constantly missing the mark. I was starting to get rather stressed out by it but I managed to calm myself and ask the mum what the images meant. The mum understood almost everything her child was relaying to me, even though the images I was being sent were making no logical sense to me whatsoever.

'Eloise tells me that her daddy used to eat with her but doesn't anymore,' I said.

'Yes, we all used to eat together as my husband wasn't working for three months but we don't now he's started working again.' Then we went off at a complete tangent.

'I keep being shown lights going on and off,' I said, not having a clue what this could mean.

'Only this morning Eloise was playing with a musical toy which says "lights on, lights off". I showed her what it meant using the kitchen light.'

'Who's on medication but has stopped taking it?' I was starting to get the impression that Eloise liked to get through discussions very quickly.

'That was me. I went back on the Pill but it made me depressed so I came off it.'

Then we went off at another tangent. 'I'm being told that you weren't feeling 100 per cent when you were wearing wellies last week!'

'I wore wellies a few weeks ago when it was raining a lot and I was feeling depressed and tearful. Eloise obviously noticed that I was distressed.'

'There is something weird about someone cutting their toenails in your house.' Anna laughed. This really seemed to strike a chord with her.

'My husband had a new toenail specially grown for him in a lab after a rugby accident and it's so tough that he has to cut it with garden shears!'

Sometimes I find it awkward delivering embarrassing information. I don't like to hold back, though. I'll tell the parents whatever I'm told by the baby I'm connecting with. It's not my job to get emotionally involved. I'm only the messenger. I'm shown information for a reason, and I'm not the one who should decide what the parent should or shouldn't hear. Honesty is always the best policy, and over the years people have grown to respect me for that. I may soften the blow if the information is of a very personal nature. If I felt I could hurt someone deeply I would choose my time to tell them what I'd been told by their child. If I'm sitting with a mum and dad and a particularly sensitive message comes through which could upset one of them I might ask the other parent to leave the room in order for me to 'spill the beans'. The last thing I want is to cause any more offence than necessary.

Two-year-old Taylor Lanning told me something about his mum, Caroline, that I thought she would be embarrassed to talk about in front of her husband, Phil. 'Is it okay if I talk to you alone, Caroline?'

'I've got no problem with you telling me something in front of Phil.'

'Well, this could be really difficult for you to hear.'

'No, it's no problem. I've got nothing to hide.'

'Well, there's a message coming through from Taylor about you shaving your fanny in the shape of a heart as a surprise for Phil!'

We all fell about laughing and Phil's face went bright red! Surprisingly, Caroline was unperturbed by my outrageous remark and stayed very cool. 'Well, you've just spoiled my surprise now!' she exclaimed. 'That was meant to be Phil's Valentine's Day present!'

I have been known to receive very important information when I'm connecting telepathically with a child. I can sometimes pick up messages incorrectly, though, and I'm aware that I can subconsciously interfere with what I'm being told and end up telling the parents something that was not exactly what the child meant me to say. When children are particularly inept at communicating with me there can be a great deal of ambiguity in their messages. Some young children can be incredibly inconsistent and their conversation can be almost impossible to follow. It can be very unsettling for both me and their parents when they begin to discuss an interesting topic and then fly off at a tangent to a completely new one.

On many occasions I've found myself embroiled in family disputes. This can be very embarrassing, especially when there are unresolved relationship issues at stake. A baby once revealed to me in front of his parents that his dad was not his real father! Generally, though, family squabbles tend to be about fairly minor details that seem to cause a lot of upset. Sometimes, for instance, babies tell me that dad has been in trouble for spending too long in the toilet or not washing the dishes properly.

I try very hard not to allow myself to get involved in these feuds, and I have been known to stop a reading if I felt it would do more harm than good to continue with it. We all have secrets from our past and sometimes it's best to keep them there. Therefore I always ask a parent before I start if there are any areas of their life that I shouldn't touch on during their reading. I can gauge from their reaction where the line is that I shouldn't cross. I don't want any parent to feel nervous during a reading. That wouldn't do anyone any good. It would unsettle them, unsettle me and ultimately unsettle their child. The calmer everyone is the better. Some of my most successful readings have occurred when the energy in the room is positive and the parents are relaxed and keen to hear what their child has to say.

Every parent I've met has had expectations. Some who come to see me are sceptics, just looking for some form of validation to justify to themselves that there is something 'out there'. They also want to see at first hand that I can do what I say I can do. They crave the proof.

Some other parents call me because they are desperate to help their child and have tried every other method. They'd do anything for their offspring so are prepared to suspend any disbelief and try to be philosophical about their situation. Why not give the baby mind reader a try? What have we got to lose? Maybe, just maybe, there is something in this?

Many parents come along thinking I can just snap my fingers and their offspring will be happy and content; the perfect child. These thoughts may be loosely based on the assumption that I can change lives overnight. I can do this, and have many times in the past, but only if I can get to the root of their child's issues almost immediately. These parents want answers and will not accept it when I tell them I can only work with the information that comes through. I'm constantly telling people that I don't do requests! I'm not a journalist. I don't have specific interview techniques. If a child wants to talk to me then they will. In fact, some have been so desperate to communicate with me that I've not even had time to take off my jacket. Usually, though, I'll try and ask them some questions and find out what's troubling them, but they are always in control. If they want to let the world know what's bothering them then they'll only do it when the time is right.

Many readings are like marathons and will take time whereas others are 100-metre sprints and over in a flash. If a child is in for the long haul then patience is a must. I've been known to take two or even three meetings to get to the bottom of certain issues surrounding a child.

Words and pictures –
how babies communicate
with me

It's taken me a few years to fathom out the code children use when they communicate with me telepathically. Not surprisingly, they use the same basic language as the spirit world, although it has a slightly different 'dialect'. I hear sounds, see images and feel thoughts and sensations, just as when I am communicating with spirits. These are put into my mind and body by the child when they send me information.

For a reading to go well, three things must happen: the child must want to communicate with me; I have to understand clearly what's been transmitted to me; and the parent has to be aware of what they are being told, and the drive to act upon it if necessary. If a reading is going well, that's because I am simply passing on exactly what I'm being given. If it's going badly then I'm obviously not picking up correctly what the child is trying to say, or I'm misinterpreting the messages I'm being sent.

When a baby is totally inept at communicating with me then it's very frustrating for everyone involved. Not every child is capable of expressing themselves, let alone telepathically, so the information that comes through in a reading can appear rather vague, be disappointing for both me and the parent and leave us both totally confused.

Over the years I've tried to read as many children as possible so that, as with any new language, I'll become as fluent as possible. It's not always easy as many children have their own idiosyncrasies. One symbol can mean a particular thing to one child and signify something totally different to another.

My goal is to help the child in whatever way possible. I've always aimed to validate that I'm actually connecting with the child through conveying specific unquestionable details about their life or their problems. There's no point telling a parent what's bothering their child or how to solve their child's problem if the parent doesn't believe the information is actually coming from them in the first place. My priority at all times is therefore to convince the parent that I am genuine and that I can do what I say I can do.

It takes a huge amount of energy to communicate telepathically with a child. I can become very tired after a reading and sometimes even during the reading if it's a particularly long or difficult one. There's no hard and fast rule as to how long a reading will last. That's up to the child. It's not unusual for a child to be totally exhausted after a particularly long encounter with me as they may also expend a great deal of energy when they communicate telepathically. I'm brought down to the child's energy level while I'm connecting with them. If I need to increase these energy levels to help the connection stay strong then I let the child steal some of my energy, which can be very draining for me.

As an emotional person, I can immediately pinpoint hurt, fear, sadness or anger and then send that message to the parent. For the child, who may rely a great deal on their emotions to express their feelings on a daily basis, it is often the easiest way for them to communicate with me. However, just because I see something in a certain context doesn't mean everyone else will see it like that. I have to be careful not to imprint my subconscious views or beliefs on a particular piece of information I receive telepathically from a child. When I'm asked to deliver a feeling of being sad or angry, I have to ensure that I do this to the same degree as the child. I try to repeat exactly what I'm being told and to do it with no more or less expression than necessary.

When I hear a voice in my head it is my voice – my mind's voice – although I fully understand who is 'doing the talking'. The child doesn't speak to me directly but they do communicate by repeating sections of conversations they've overheard, which they've deemed important or life-changing. They can do this almost to the exact word. They seem to have knowledge of discussions rather than an actual understanding of words. When I hear these conversations in my mind I'll be told in picture form who has said what, or the words will come out of that particular person's mouth.

Children also build up pictures of events in my mind's eye if they feel it's necessary. If I don't understand something and let the child know, they may repeat the image, and if I'm still finding it difficult to interpret they add 'bonus material' where images may be embellished with a sound bite or a 'feeling'. Babies sometimes show me things that I can relate to in order to clarify the image, sound or feeling they are sending me. That can be very weird, especially if my mum or dad or a private detail from my life suddenly pops up during a reading when I'm with a child who's a complete stranger!

I see these images in colour so sometimes colours change in order for a child to help me validate a message. All I'm actually doing is repeating, as best I can, what I'm seeing, feeling or hearing from the child, and delivering my interpretation of that information as quickly and clearly as possible to the parent. My accuracy is limited only by the strength and clarity of the telepathic connection I have with the child.

Some of the information that comes through in readings is easy for me to interpret whereas other pieces are symbolic. My accuracy comes from the experience I've gained over the years in interpreting messages and my general knowledge of the techniques a child may use to communicate with me.

Some children show me objects, symbols or pictures of scenes in a totally non-literal way, and this can be really confusing. I've been shown balloons to signify parties or anniversaries and glass to indicate windows or mirrors. Polished shoes have meant anything from a policeman, soldier or fireman to anyone in the services, but they have also been known to signify new shoes! I've been shown large steering wheels by children who were trying to tell me that someone drove a bus or lorry, while a piece of shiny metal has been used to represent a ring or watch, even a key ring. More often than not it's down to me and the child's parents to work out what their offspring is trying to say.

I was once with a 10-month-old boy called Marcus whose mum, Anna, had got in touch. During the reading Marcus kept showing me a watch face that read five to or five past the hour. I was stumped because I was getting no other information from Marcus. Luckily, Anna understood the message clearly as this was the time she always woke Marcus and showed him the face on the clock above his bed! I also recall Marcus showing me an image of four chairs, which he surrounded with negative energy. This was cryptic but I knew from experience that this is a child's way of showing me that something 'isn't right' and is either broken or needs changing. Anna's response didn't surprise me when she mentioned that she and her husband had recently discussed changing the dining room chairs!

When a child wants to talk about their family they usually show me an image of a family tree. If there's been a divorce or death then the energy will be negative around the place on the tree where that family member would normally be placed. Marcus sent me this very image when I sat with him but there was also a message coming through on the back of it about his grandmother. Had his grandmother died or been divorced? Anna later confirmed that her dad's ex-wife, Joan, regularly looked after Marcus!

Luckily, there are stock images that every child seems to use, and these are easy to interpret. I may be shown a Ferris wheel to signify the London Eye, or a day at a theme park or maybe an aircraft to describe a trip abroad. A taxi is always shown as a black or dark blue car, and a police car is always white. I can get confused between an ambulance and an ice-cream van, though, as both are shown as white vans with a funny noise associated with them!

I do make errors of judgement during readings and get things wrong. I may overanalyse an image, and that can make me look stupid. Sometimes something is really just what it is. A doll is a doll or a fork is a fork. I also find it hard not to over-interpret messages, especially if I feel I need to impress a sceptical parent.

It's fairly easy to interpret names as I usually hear them quite clearly in my head. Sometimes I just get the start of a name or an initial but that's usually enough for the parents to grasp who their child is talking about. There have been times when I've been shown a symbol to validate a name. I was once sent an image by a child of a teddy bear for 'Ted', and I've even been shown a picture of a crane to validate 'Derek'! Generally, if I hear a 'J' or I'm shown that initial in conjunction with the image of a man's silhouette then it's pretty obvious that the child is trying to tell me about possibly 'Jim' or 'John', or if it's a woman's image, maybe 'Joyce' or 'Joan'. Names like 'Philip' normally come through to me by their dominant sound, 'ph', or I could be shown that sound as 'F'. I usually get full names but that doesn't always happen. I do get nicknames too, but not as often as proper full names.

I was once shown a picture in my mind of 'The Simpsons'. Luckily, the mum who was sitting with me at the time quickly acknowledged that I was being told this because her husband's nickname was Homer! A little boy, on a television show I was recording, showed me a picture in my mind of the band Aerosmith. I was unsure as to what this meant, but as soon as I mentioned this to his mum she told me that his name was Tyler, the same name as that band's lead singer!

Small children know about numbers. They understand that numbers have a place in the world but not necessarily their significance. If I'm shown a number, my subconscious will help me interpret what it means, especially if it's to validate particular days, months or years. A number may also be used to validate a place of residence. Sometimes I get only the first digit of a larger number. Maybe the child doesn't know it or has forgotten it. If this happens I go back to the child and ask them for an image to help me confirm what they are trying to portray. If I know there is a second digit and I'm then shown the picture of a house, I have to rely on the parent to validate a house number.

During readings I have also been told PIN numbers for bank cards and codes for house alarms. I'm not shown the numbers as numbers. I'm actually shown an image of where the parents put their fingers on the key pad, so putting a finger on the top right of the pad indicates number three, whereas placing a finger at the bottom left corner tells me that it's number seven. This may sound weird but remember your child may watch you when you're at the bank or is sitting beside you in their pushchair when you come home and undo your house alarm.

Not everything that comes through will relate to a parent. I may get a message about a friend or relative. This can be confusing, especially if the parent I'm sitting with has less knowledge of that person than their child has. Sometimes I become confused between family members. I may say, 'Your baby is telling me about his younger brother,' when the child is actually talking about his older brother or even himself.

Some babies give me part-messages, thinking that I'll readily understand the rest. They try and use my knowledge and life experiences to embellish their messages. I've always found that it's best, though, to tell the parent exactly what I'm being shown. I call it a 'Ronseal reading' – I do exactly what it says on the tin!

I was once with a little boy who kept giving me a tight feeling around my throat. It was as if I was being choked. 'Your son doesn't like anything tight around his throat,' I told his mum.

'Yes, that's correct,' she replied. 'He always seems to cry when he wears anything that is anywhere near his neck.'

The messages of 'energy' I'm sent are fairly easy for me to interpret. I just use the feeling, place it in my body and I'll quickly understand why the child is sending me this information. It's not always cut and dried, though, as a pain in my ear may indicate an ear infection but could also have something to do with a new pair of earrings or maybe a pair of spectacles that need adjusting! If I get stuck I go back to the child and ask them for more help. They will usually elaborate on the first image so that I can make the message fit properly.

When I deal with images, thoughts, feelings and sounds during a reading it can be a huge amount to handle all at once. Some messages throw me off the scent. Sometimes children don't speak to me in a logical fashion and jump around from one message to another. Other children have very short attention spans or think tangentially – I may be talking about an event and then I'm suddenly shown a horse or a piece of cake! This can be very alarming, especially if I think that these messages could be connected!

A good reading is one where all these techniques come together. It's one where I successfully put the various images, feelings and sound bites into a coherent form which is easily understood by the parent. There have been times during readings when it may look like I'm just pulling things out of thin air or trying to make things fit into place, but it's definitely not what's going on in my head.

I've found that children can read their parents' minds. When I'm told something about a parent's past it is shown from the mum or dad's perspective. It's as if I'm in the mum or dad's head, looking out through their eyes. I can sense everything they have sensed. This can be very alarming for me if a parent's been sexually abused as a child or maybe attacked or even raped at some point.

Something that's not important to me and I feel is not significant to the reading will occasionally pop up from nowhere, because it's significant to the child. I've learnt never to dismiss these little moments as they can be incredibly important to the whole reading.

I was giving a reading to a little boy called Dominic one day. He kept showing me that his mum had hurt her tummy while she was pregnant, and this had caused her to be terribly overprotective of him. A second image also came through of Dominic in a cot having breathing difficulties.

'You obviously remember the day when you hurt your stomach while you were pregnant?' I asked his mum. She seemed shocked at my revelation.

'Yes, I worried that I'd damaged my son.'

'Well, you seem to be upsetting him more now because I'm being told that you have been panicking about his breathing and worrying that he'll be a cot death baby.' She looked at me and smiled. I continued: 'Your son knows about your fears and they are upsetting him. Your anxiety will rub off on him if you are not careful. I can feel this from the energy Dominic is sending me as I connect with him.'

'I'd hate to think that I'm upsetting my son.'

There have been times when readings have been astoundingly accurate, with amazing information coming through. I met one little girl whose messages helped her mum to change her life.

I arranged to meet with Debbie and George Wilson at their friend's home in Dumbarton. Debbie had brought their daughter, Cameron, along to see me. Cameron was sitting on her mum's knee when I arrived, and as I walked into the room I noticed that she was wearing a very pretty dress. I immediately commented on it because it appeared to me to be very long.

Debbie and George had travelled a great distance to see me and I could feel an air of expectation in the room. I don't like it when parents get themselves worked up before they meet with me, though I can understand that they are nervous. I appreciate that they want answers or need to find the solution to one or maybe more of their problems.

Debbie explained why she had asked for my help. 'We are unhappy and feel that Cameron is too. We think she wants to let us know what's troubling her.'

'Now, I can tell you that she is really easy to connect with but I'm not too sure how good she is at telling me things yet. Let's take it slowly. I want to do my best for you so there's no need to rush things, is there?'

'No. We just need some answers. We have all the time to get them if needs be.'

I began to tune in to Cameron, and the information started coming through quite easily. The first message was simple to understand. 'Cameron tells me she's been having a problem with her neck and her hips.'

'Yes, she has. That was the beginning of her problems. Should I tell you more?'

'No, absolutely not! Just answer "yes" or "no" unless I specifically ask you for some piece of the jigsaw that I'm not getting from your daughter.'

'I'm sorry.'

'There's no need to apologize. This is the way I work. Now,' I continued, 'there is something coming through that seems really weird to me. Cameron tells me that she has one leg longer than the other. Her left leg is shorter than her right. This has got something to do with her sore hips.'

There was a deathly silence. Debbie and George looked at each other, then they both looked at me. Debbie lifted up Cameron's dress and I nearly died of shock. She had a plaster cast on each leg and a metal bar was holding one apart from the other. So there was a reason for the rather long dress after all!

'When Cameron was nine months old I noticed that her neck was clicking and I took her to see the doctor,' explained Debbie. 'He did some tests and diagnosed that she had a congenital dislocated hip. I'd no idea that she has one leg longer than the other. I'll need to speak to the doctor about that. Maybe she is trying to tell you that after her hips were positioned and reset by the hospital one has healed and moved into place and the other has yet to reset in the socket. The ligaments and muscles sometimes take time to form and stabilize the ball and socket joint.'

'No, I'm correct. Her right leg is longer than the left. It's got nothing to do with resetting muscles or ligaments. It's just so.' I took a few minutes to think this through. 'Is this problem hereditary?'

'No. She was just such a big baby that the doctors say she may have injured herself in my womb because she couldn't turn around or move. She was nearly 10 pounds when she was born.'

'Cameron tells me that she has an older sister who is six and whose name begins with the letter "K".'

'Yes, that's true. Her name is Kelsy.'

'Look, I can talk to you about details like this all day long. Why are you really here to see me?'

'We need to know how Cameron feels about her problems.'

'I don't want to appear rude,' I said, 'but I'm being made very aware that you and George seem to be the cause of most of them. You need to leave her alone and stop mollycoddling her. She's accepted the fact that she has problems. You haven't. She needs you to leave her alone and let her get on with it.'

'Well, that's going to be difficult,' replied Debbie. 'I don't want her to hurt herself. I'm frightened that I'm going to let her down.'

'Look, you are letting her down by the way you're treating her now. She doesn't want this. She wants to get on with her life. It's up to you if you listen to these messages or not but I know what Cameron wants and you both know that now too.' Debbie and George held hands. George looked anxious and Debbie was tearful.

'Cameron tells me that George is a lorry driver,' I added.

'Yes, that's what he does for a living.'

'There's a lot of information coming through from Cameron about her bedroom. I'd like to talk to you about that. I feel that this is her way of validating this reading.'

'Yes, we'd love to know what she thinks.'

'Well, I'm being told about a cream bear on her bed and terracotta walls and carpet. There's also something coming through about your back door having a broken pane of glass. It's the one in the bottom corner of the six panes.'

'We need to get that fixed!'

'Why can't she play with the Hoover?' I asked.

'I don't want her to play with something like that,' Debbie replied.

'I mean the toy Hoover in the wardrobe in the spare room. The Dyson.'

'Oh my God. How do you know about that? How does Cameron know about that? She's never seen it. It's her sister's plastic toy Dyson. That's utterly amazing!'

'Listen, Debbie. Babies read your mind. It's a fact. It may sound nuts but they do. Cameron knows about the Dyson because you know about the Dyson. She wants to play with it. This will help her to feel just like everyone else. This may sound like I'm giving you a hard time but you need to hear what I'm hearing.'

'I'm listening to you,' replied Debbie. 'It's hard to take this all in but I'm listening.'

Cameron continued to give me information. She told me about her granny in great detail, and then complained that she was fed up with eating bananas!

Debbie called me a year later. 'I just had to get in touch. Since we met you, Cameron has taken life in her stride. We've followed your advice and left her to get on with it. Within days she was crawling up the stairs in her cast and pulling herself onto furniture. She couldn't even put her feet on the ground but she used her upper body to pull herself up. She's developed so much better since we let her be. I'm so pleased we listened to you. Without any shadow of a doubt you have helped to bring our daughter on leaps and bounds. She also loves her toy Dyson.'

'I'm over the moon,' I replied. 'What's been happening with the bananas?'

'She's eating other fruits now. She loves strawberries.'

I was concerned about Cameron's health and asked Debbie to let me know how things were.

'You were correct – her right leg is longer than the left. Our doctor is dumbfounded. It's amazing that you knew that.'

We all like our comfort zones. They make us feel good and safe. Comfort zones may also limit us, though, and stop us from moving on with our lives. To be able to move forward psychically, I've learnt to take a good, honest look at my daily routine and also my comfort zones. More radically, I have also changed the way that I think about, or perceive, a child. I realize that I will only be able to receive clear pictures and messages from a baby's brain if I am in total control of my feelings and have peace and balance in my life.

A child will not communicate with me telepathically all the time. Babies will only connect when they feel the need to do so. There will be a time and a place but it will always be on their terms. My job is to be ready to interpret the information and act upon it responsibly.

Putting it all together

So a child's acting up? First, I stay calm. Then I finish off what I'm doing, if that's possible, and try to clear my head. I try not to be drawn into the child's control drama and also not to worry about who is around me or what is going on. Clearing myself of outside influences and stimulants – such as the noise from the radio or television and people's chatter – is crucial. I then start talking slowly and calmly to the child, using this time to find my balance and to take as much control of the situation as I can. I go to the place in my head where I find it easiest to receive images and feelings from a child. If I block myself the messages will not come through, no matter how strong they are. I try to breathe slowly and deeply. This usually helps the child recognize that I am not taking part in their drama and will not let them destroy me with their stress.

I then let the child know that I am ready. If I feel the need, I work at their eye level and actually tell them. It's best, though, to stay at least a couple of feet away from the child so I don't start getting involved with their energy. If they are crying or acting up I just let them burn themselves out. Children still communicate telepathically whilst they are having tantrums! By this point I'm usually totally in my zone and ready to receive messages. I don't worry about what's going on around me as I always have an awareness of any potential risk to me or the child. By concentrating on the child's telepathic messages I am not totally blocking out everything that's going on. My inner self will always protect me. It's all part of my instinct as a human being.

As I connect I take each image and try to decipher the message as quickly as I can. I have to be on guard, just in case I use my subconscious to distort the messages. A child may wish to tell me something I already know so I try not to be too dismissive. It's what I don't know or understand that's important!

Children have a tendency to hold on to things that are really bothering them so I try not to let that trouble me. Just because their parents said 'no' to the new toy car or the trip to the zoo doesn't mean that the child won't mention it again. Usually, if the parent is okay with it and the reading is going well, it's good to let them know that they may get their wish at some point in the future, although now isn't the right time.

I would never patronize a child, ever. They may be only young but a quick explanation as to why I did something or why their parents reacted to something in a certain fashion really helps calm a situation down. I keep things clear and simple though. I always sing from the same hymn sheet as their parents, no matter how difficult that may be. Consistency is everything.

I let children be fully aware when I understand the message that's been sent to me and remember to thank them. At that point they'll move on to the next piece of information if they feel the need to do so. If I don't fully understand what a child is trying to tell me then I let them know. If I don't then I usually get very confused. One piece of detail may lead to another so I always keep this chain of imagery as clear and logical as I can.

I've always to remember, though, not to shoot the messenger! Just because a child tells me that their daddy is having an affair with mummy's best friend doesn't mean that I will show my reaction to the child, even if this is being explained to me in the middle of a television studio!

If something important is revealed to me then I stay calm. If I didn't then I could scare the child and they might not open up to me again. Obviously I would never dream of spilling the beans in order to make good television and to shock someone. If I'm told a piece of sensitive information then I act accordingly and would discuss the issue with each parent separately to avoid any hurt, confusion or divorce proceedings!

I met Wilma and Tam McDonald and their son Liam at a motel just outside Glasgow. They had travelled all the way from the Highlands to see me. Wilma had called to arrange the reading but had told me nothing about Liam or what problems he had. She was very concerned about her son, that was for sure, but I didn't know what these concerns were.

When I arrived the McDonalds were waiting in their room. It wasn't easy trying to tune in to Liam. He was tired after his long journey, and I guess I was really the last person he wanted to see. He was fascinated by his new environment and wanted to play constantly with the television remote control or jump on the double bed. To any outsider he seemed like a normal, happy, two-year-old boy but I soon became aware that he was nothing of the sort.

Once Liam calmed down and was playing quietly on the bed with his dad and a few of his toys he began to open up to me. 'Liam tells me that he has a few issues,' I said, looking at Wilma and Tam. 'There seem to be two main problems here: one is sleeping and the other is eating. I'm not sure yet how we can solve both but I've got a fair idea so let's talk that out.' Liam was sending me some very clear images, which I realized could upset his parents.

'Okay, I'm possibly going to hurt your feelings here but I really feel that Liam is scared to sleep. It's almost like he's fearful that you'll abandon him. Please don't feel that I'm calling you bad parents. I'm just telling you what's coming through.'

'Well, that makes sense,' replied Wilma. 'He's always upset when either of us leaves him. He's very clingy. I won't take anything you say personally, Derek. Please just tell us what Liam needs.' I could sense that Wilma was desperate for some help and guidance. Tam was very quiet. He just looked over at me and nodded.

'Liam's also saying to me that he's had problems breathing. It's as if he had trouble with his lungs when he was a baby.' I waited to hear Wilma's response. She was staring at me and had a smile on her face. I was obviously hitting on something that meant a great deal to Liam and his parents.

I went back to Liam and connected with him. I could sense that he now knew I was his friend and was there to help. The images started to flow and our telepathic connection became very strong. I decided to tell Wilma and Tam what I was now being told. 'Does this make sense to you? I'm being shown two images: one's of a hospital and the other's a blue tube. These two images are very strong and are definitely connected. This particular blue tube was part of an electrical unit in the hospital, possibly a ventilator or monitor. I'm not 100 per cent on that but I'm certain that you'll know what I'm talking about. Something was sucked out of this blue tube. I can sense suction. I'm being shown by Liam that this place unsettled him and is still haunting him to this day. He's uncertain about how he should really deal with these images and feelings.'

There was silence in the room. You could have heard a pin drop. I could see that Tam was losing his composure for the first time. He seemed to squirm as he lay on the bed. Wilma then began to tell me their story. She explained how after 10 years of marriage she'd eventually got pregnant and had given birth to a stillborn baby called Scott.

This was a devastating time for Wilma and Tam but they vowed to keep trying to have a child. When Wilma got pregnant for the second time, two-and-a-half years later, they were both thrilled. It wasn't an easy pregnancy, however. Wilma had problems with high blood pressure, which led to kidney failure, so Liam had to be delivered early. 'Liam was born three months premature,' explained Wilma. 'He was 26 weeks old when I gave birth to him and weighed just one pound six ounces. He was the size of my hand, and was in hospital for the first six months of his life. I was told that it was touch and go.'

I was then told something astounding by Liam. I just had to tell Wilma and Tam. 'Wilma, did you know that Liam was actually a twin and that he has a baby sister in the spirit world?' Neither Wilma nor Tam seemed taken aback by this comment. 'Well, another psychic told me that so I'm not surprised. I've always felt that, strangely enough. The psychic also said that I'd lost a daughter.'

I was stunned. I now knew, without question, what Liam's issues were. The jigsaw was beginning to come together. 'So why am I being shown the blue tube?' I asked.

'He had a blue tube that kept him breathing. It took mucus out of his lungs. It was linked to his ventilator. He was in his incubator for four months,' Tam replied. 'That's spot on.'

'Well, I now realize what your problem is. Liam feels abandoned because he was in the hospital for all that time when he should have been with his mum and dad. It's now time to explain things a little more to Liam. Once you start to do that he'll be fine. You need to make sure he understands when you are going out, why you are going out and how long you'll be. He needs to know that you'll never just disappear and that you'll both always come back. That's what's panicking him and he's not sleeping because of it.'

'Well, he seems to be okay when he's sleeping in the lounge but when we put him in his room he just starts acting up.'

I was fazed by Wilma's comment. It just didn't seem to stack up with what Liam was showing me. 'I don't see that at all, Wilma. He's telling me that when he's in his room he feels great. It's when he's with you in the lounge that he's acting up.'

'No, it's exactly the opposite,' Tam insisted.

I was still adamant that I was correct. 'Liam's telling me that he's fine when he's upstairs but not when he's downstairs.'

'Exactly,' said Tam. 'You're thinking that his bedroom's upstairs and the lounge is downstairs. They aren't – it's the opposite way around! Our lounge is upstairs and Liam's bedroom is downstairs. So we are both right!' I was speechless. This was undoubtedly proving that Liam was communicating with me telepathically.

'Thank goodness we sorted that one out. I thought I was going mad for a second,' I added. 'It was my fault, though. Subconsciously I took his message and immediately assumed something that was incorrect. You can't blame me that much, though. How many houses are designed like that? Not many I bet!' Both Wilma and Tam had a chuckle. They didn't seem as nervous now but I knew there were still a few issues that had to be sorted out before the reading was over.

'We've always let him sleep on the couch and then put him in his room when we go to bed. That's when he starts to act up.' I listened to what Tam had to say and went back to Liam. He was very keen on letting me know what was troubling him.

'Liam's just told me that he wakes between midnight and 1am nearly every morning. It's like clockwork. You could set your alarm by him.'

'That's right. It's driving us mad,' replied Wilma.

'That's because he's reminded about a procedure that would happen in the hospital at that time in the night. He tells me that he's been so used to it he now wakes up thinking it's still going to happen.'

'I can't believe that. It seems very weird but the time you've mentioned is correct,' Tam added. He seemed perplexed and worried by this.

'Well, you'll need to bring him into your room for a bit. Liam wants to be with you at night. Let him sleep on the couch until you're ready to go to bed then take him into your room and put his bed there too. This sleeping arrangement will end when you've decorated the room with the blue carpet, which I believe could be your living room. That's when he'll sleep in his own room all night.'

'Thank you for that,' Tam replied. 'The blue carpet is in the living room and we are planning to redecorate soon. Why do we have to wait until the room is ready before Liam is prepared to sleep on his own?'

I thought for a moment and went back to Liam. 'I'm afraid I can't answer that one. Maybe Liam knows something you don't.'

There was more information coming through and I was conscious of the fact that Liam could get tired, so instead of waiting to find out more about the sleeping arrangements I continued with the reading. 'I get the impression that he's not eating.'

'Yes, it's a nightmare,' Wilma replied.

'I don't want to sound bigheaded but when you leave here today you will not have one more issue with Liam's eating.'

'How can you be so sure?' Tam asked.

'All you have to do is reduce the portions you give him. Now, don't get me wrong, you've to keep the total amount that Liam eats the same.'

'I don't understand,' Wilma said.

'I'm being told by Liam that he gets panicky when he sees too much food on his plate so you need to play a game with him. When it's time for tea make the amount of food that he needs to eat but give it to him over two or three servings. Each plate of food will look smaller than a huge meal and he'll feel a sense of achievement when he's actually finished what's on his plate. Remember to praise him. That's important. When he's eaten what you've given him go and get some more and present that to him. Keep going until he's eaten his entire meal.'

'So he gets scared about too much food being on his plate?'

'Yes, he does. It sounds daft but at some point in his life he's seen or heard or even felt something that's triggered this complex. In time he will get over it but you'll just have to work with him. Start tonight. You'll see immediately that it works, I promise you.' Wilma and Tam looked surprised but I knew by this time that I'd won them over and they would give it a go. What had they got to lose anyway?

There was more to come from Liam though. 'Liam's telling me that he's frightened of blood. I also feel that he's got a complex about anything to do with people touching his feet.'

'Absolutely!' exclaimed Wilma. 'When Liam was a baby they took blood from his feet when he was in the incubator. He won't let me anywhere near them.'

'What was it like when Liam eventually came home?' I asked Wilma.

'We'd all been through such an awful time. It was fantastic when we brought him home. We played it low-key though. I kept it out of the papers. I just suddenly, for the first time, really felt like Liam's mum.' Wilma then went on to say that she blamed herself for Liam's problems and kept asking herself where she had gone wrong. I felt for her because some of her problems were still here. 'Liam has chronic lung disease,' she told me, 'which means that when he gets a cold he has to go to the hospital for up to a week at a time.' I was sorry to hear that. It was sad that this little boy had such a cross to bear but I was confident that his life was going to change for the better after this reading. As if by magic, Liam began to tell me about something that was really upsetting him. 'Liam tells me that he doesn't want to have a potty anymore. You've to bin it. He wants to sit on the loo like his mum and dad. Could you sort that out for him?'

'Of course we can,' replied Tam. 'We've got a great deal to work on when we get home but it's no problem. I'll buy him one of those little seats that fit onto the loo on Monday when we get back home.'

I heard from Wilma a few months later. She was ecstatic. 'We did throw away that potty two days after we met you and it worked a treat. Unbelievable! After your reading it was just fantastic; everything worked within days. Liam started to eat and sleep and our lives have been totally transformed. We can't thank you enough.'

Some months earlier I'd worked on a feature for the *Daily Mail*, where I'd met three mums and done readings for their children. Just as I was starting to think that the feature would never appear, I received a telephone call telling me that the article would be on the front page of the next day's paper, with a two-page spread inside. I was flabbergasted.

The next morning my life was about to change forever. I couldn't believe I was on the front page. The headline read: 'Amazing story of the Scot who can read babies' minds'. Beside it was a rather dashing picture of me. Inside there was another picture of me, and each mum and her child had been photographed beside a written description of their reading. It was all great stuff.

I had asked for my telephone number and email address to be printed at the end of the feature so that anyone in the media world could get in touch. I had no idea, though, that I would be inundated with requests from parents from all over the world! My phone was red hot. Twelve TV production companies also called and wanted to meet with me. I was overjoyed.

I was contacted by Living TV, who were interested in offering me my own series. Before they actually signed me, they wanted me to contact each and every production company that had shown an interest in working with me and ask them to tender for the contract to produce the series.

In the meantime, Living TV offered me the job of resident psychic on *I'm Famous and Frightened*. I started working on the show a few days later. At the Edinburgh TV Festival I found out that TalkBack Productions had won the tender and would be producing my series. I was thrilled.

I was told that I was to be taken off *I'm Famous and Frightened* because they didn't want the Living audience to associate me with talking to the dead when I was going to be recording a baby show for them. I was disappointed but understood their reasons. Strangely, someone somewhere was trying to tell me that my relationship with Living TV wasn't going to run as smoothly as I thought. When the phone rang the next morning I wasn't in the least bit surprised to hear from Mentorn TV Productions. I knew they were disappointed to have missed out on the Living TV deal. They asked me to meet them to talk about doing a documentary.

I met Viv McGrath, an executive producer for the company. Viv had been having a great deal of success with a series called *Extraordinary People*, and thought I would be ideal material for her next show. Viv and I immediately hit it off. She was excited about working with me on her documentary series, so when we met with Justine Kershaw at Channel Five that afternoon, Viv was hoping for her idea to get a seal of approval from one of Five's top commissioning editors. I was on a roll that day, and once I saw that Justine was pregnant there was no holding me back! We got on very well and I liked Justine's style.

After the meeting, I went out with Viv and some others and got absolutely smashed. I don't drink but on this one occasion I was legless. In the morning I had one of my worst headaches ever, so I wasn't exactly in the right frame of mind to answer a rather frantic call from Viv. She told me to sit down as she had some amazing news. Five wanted to sign me up for two years and to give me my own series! I was still drunk so I asked Viv to repeat what she had just told me. Was I hearing things or, worse still, was I dreaming? When the news sunk in, I felt numb. This was the best news that I'd had for six years. There was a slight cloud on my horizon, though. What on earth was I going to tell Living TV?

Elizabeth's story – a need for security

Before I signed my exclusive deal with Five in October 2004 they auditioned me under the most extreme and unusual circumstances. I was taken to a production company's headquarters in London and asked to read 13 young children, one by one, over two days. The test really exhausted me but I fully understood that Five had to make sure they were getting exactly what they were paying for. I had no problem with that although some of the children proved to be a bit of a handful!

I met with Susan Clarke and her daughter, Elizabeth, on the Saturday afternoon of that eventful weekend, and they proved to be a very interesting duo. The minute I walked into the room I connected with Elizabeth, who was playing on the floor at her mum's feet. She seemed to be very upset with her mum and I could feel her anger. 'Elizabeth wants to know why you didn't allow her to have make-up on today,' I said to Susan. Susan nodded. I went back to Elizabeth and asked her to tell me more. 'She tells me that she had make-up on during the week, either Wednesday or Thursday, but that you didn't allow her to put it on today.'

'Well, I knew we were coming here today, so I didn't want her to have make-up on in front of the cameras.' Susan looked surprised by my revelation. She smiled at me nervously.

Elizabeth then told me a few more details about her life. 'Elizabeth's just said to me that she has a brother but that they have different dads.'

'That's correct,' Susan replied. 'How did you know that?' Maybe she'd forgotten that I was a baby mind reader! 'I think you are amazing,' Susan said. 'I am just absolutely stunned because everything was spot on.'

I hadn't been given enough time to do a full reading. I'd been told that one family would be chosen for a further reading scheduled later on that week, and I hoped that it would be Susan and Elizabeth. If they were picked by the production director, this meeting would be filmed in their own home.

Sure enough, Susan and Elizabeth were selected for the second reading. I met with the Clarkes two days later in their home in Manchester. I could immediately sense that Elizabeth was desperate to communicate with me. I was certain she had issues that she wanted resolving. I just hoped I would understand what she wanted to say to me. This was her chance to be heard and I didn't want to blow it.

I started to tune in to Elizabeth almost immediately. 'Elizabeth is telling me that she was a little unsettled last night. Have you noticed how she gets very annoyed, arrogant, upset and angry?' Susan nodded. 'She tells me that this anger just comes and then suddenly she's okay.'

'Yes, the minute Elizabeth wakes up I feel really stressed because I think, oh my God, she's up. What's she going to start off with today? Elizabeth kicks, punches and bites me.' Susan began to get upset. 'Sometimes she head-butts me. She's always screaming and having tantrums. Getting Elizabeth to sit down and eat her food is a problem. If she'd been my first child, I would never have had another one.'

I could see that Susan had some serious issues, and she continued to tell me about them. 'I started taking Elizabeth to a drop-in centre. The first day she went she attacked four kids. I spent about an hour there and I left. I was too embarrassed.' Susan was obviously upset by her problems. I was then sent a rush of emotions from Elizabeth.

'She tells me that she just wants to slap you. Do you understand me?' I replied. 'One of the reasons why she gets so annoyed is because you are so indecisive about what you want to do with your life. You have to become more focused. She is picking up on your indecision and it's making her feel very insecure.' I looked at Susan and she stared back at me. I hoped she was listening. 'Elizabeth's telling me that she's confused about which bedroom she's to sleep in. She also tells me that each bedroom is just a mess. Please don't think I'm being rude but she's taking me upstairs psychically and telling me that the bedroom above my head is a mess, and there is a horrendous emotional situation for her upstairs that's to do with the mess. It's the bedroom that looks out onto the back garden, the one with the window that doesn't open properly. Elizabeth tells me there is a mattress on the floor and a cupboard with an open door because things are falling out.'

'That's completely correct,' Susan replied. There was more to come though. I could feel Elizabeth sending me more and more messages. 'She's also concerned about why there are so many women around her. You are discussing your private business with these women. She feels she's losing your compassion and the love and security she should be getting. You are chatting to too many other people and not spending enough time with Elizabeth. Spend more time with her and less time with all the people around you. Don't have so many friends around over the next week. One of the reasons why she's getting so angry is to let you know that you need to listen to her. Do you understand that?'

'Trust me, I just want to have a normal life,' replied Susan. I want a normal day, with a normal 18-month-old child. I want to see the family happy.'

The reading then went off on another tangent. Elizabeth was in control so I just went with it. 'You've been having chest problems but keeping them from your family; pains in your chest,' I said. 'Can I continue with this because your daughter is concerned about it?'

'Yes,' Susan replied.

'You've also been worried about a lump or a problem with a breast.'

'Yes.' There was stunned silence.

I felt I might have overstepped the mark but Susan let me continue. 'Your daughter is concerned because you've not gone to the doctor about this. Some discharge oozes from the nipple, and that is scaring Elizabeth.' Susan nodded. 'You have to go to the doctor and sort these problems out,' I added. Elizabeth was sending her mummy a serious message so I had to press home the point.

'How personal can I get?' I asked. 'Can I whisper in your ear?' I then whispered, 'You've been raped.'

'Yes,' replied Susan. She began to look rather shocked.

'Can I say it out loud?' I was worried that Susan might not want me to spill the beans to the production crew who obviously didn't have a clue what we were talking about. I looked at Susan and she nodded her approval.

'Well, you've been raped and your daughter is very concerned about that as well because, yet again, you are not dealing with it. She started getting upset when she was in your tummy when you were seven months pregnant because she knew there was a lot of energy in your private area left over from the rape, and therefore she was scared to come out of your womb,' I said.

I could feel Elizabeth's energy pulling back. I thought she'd said everything she wanted to say. She was obviously exhausted by this event but I knew deep down that she had enjoyed telling me all about her traumas.

'Oh my God. Did you hear what he just said?' Susan asked her sister. Susan looked stunned. It was time to quickly go over the reading and let Susan know what her daughter wanted her to do over the next few days.

'Right, so you are going to see the doctor and get your breast looked at, and you are also going to take time to think about your rape and, if need be, get help from a professional for that too. You need to get your head sorted out by people who know what they are talking about,' I said. 'Over the next seven days you are going to reduce the contact you've got with your family. They'll be okay with that because they want to help you. You are going to spend more time with your daughter too. And remember to fix the bedroom. She just wants it to be like any little girl wants her room.

You have to give her space and let her have her things around her.'

The reading had been a success but the rest was up to Susan. What did she think of the reading? 'This has all been overwhelming,' she said. She was shaking and had to sit outside to get some fresh air. 'It really touched me. You're so right, upstairs is a mess. All around the bedroom is a mess. The minute Elizabeth comes into that bedroom things fall down on her. The window doesn't work when she tries to push it up. She gets frustrated with that. I'm going to spend more time with Elizabeth and give her more hugs and kisses and try to put her to bed myself at night.' Susan was beginning to appear much more positive about things. 'I'm going to sort out the bedroom. I didn't realize that my problems were affecting Elizabeth so much until you said it. I've got to start taking care of myself so Elizabeth will be more relaxed and at ease. That will be the best thing for all of us, especially Elizabeth.'

Susan's spirit made me so happy. The ball was firmly in her court, though, and she was the only one who could begin to change her daughter's life for the better. I said my goodbyes and left. The crew would be back in seven days to find out how Susan and Elizabeth had got on.

One week later the results were utterly astounding. Was Elizabeth now acting like a normal 18-month-old little girl? 'In one week my whole life has changed,' said Susan.

'Last week it was like a storm and now look at this peace and calm! Derek told me to spend time with Elizabeth and sort out the bedroom. That same evening I started doing it. I realized in the same evening − not even a couple of days later but the same evening − I could feel the difference!' said Susan. 'I saw a change in Elizabeth. She was much bubblier. She skipped across the bed. I thought, "Great, he's right. It's working! I'll go and tackle another problem." So I tried to spend more time with Elizabeth, singing little nursery rhymes and things, and that child was just so happy. She was laughing and giggling.' Susan seemed really pleased. 'The same evening I went straight to the doctor and told him about the pains. He examined me and gave me this form to take to the hospital. I've got to go for a chest X-ray. Now, as you can see, Elizabeth is very calm. It's making life easier for everybody in the house! Thank you Derek.'

Five were pleased with the results of my test and so was I. It was time to look forward now and for some hard work. I had a television series to make for Five, some babies to help and lives to change. I was looking forward to this next challenge.

Jacob's story – the terrible twos

When a young child cries, can't sleep, won't eat, has temper tantrums or is generally restless, the parents' first thought is that they are doing something 'wrong'. Despite the best of intentions, these real issues can cause a great deal of stress in any family. I do what I can for parents and their offspring but sometimes I feel under a great deal of pressure to help put things 'right'. I can't change the world. I can only give advice and then it's up to parents whether or not they take that advice on board.

I believe that a child generally stops communicating psychically when they start to develop their ego at around the age of two or three. The advent of the ego is the beginning of discord and disharmony. These negative attributes kick in as soon as the child develops a sense of being separated from their baby world. They're suddenly knowledgeable about being a separate entity in a world of separate things.

After that it's a slippery slope. The child begins to become aware of their life-support system, the person they have bonded with, usually their mother or father. This person has nursed them, gives them food and comfort, praises and plays with them and ultimately loves them. When the parent begins chastising the child, the tone of their voice raises fear in the child, and can lead to the terrible twos, something every parent dreads. These toddler tantrums make everyone's life a misery.

When I met with Jacob, he was in a league of his own. His mum and dad had tried everything, but nothing was helping. Jacob's relentless outbursts and bad behaviour were driving his parents to despair. When Jacob got going his dad described him as 'Damian'.

Jacob and his four-year-old brother, Samuel, lived in Derby with their mum and dad Nicky and Stephen Woodroffe-Bird. Nicky and Stephen were finding Jacob very hard to handle. Jacob was constantly hitting Samuel, as well as kicking and biting him. Although Nicky and Stephen had tried everything – books, videos and even a visit to the doctor – nothing was working for them. When Jacob wasn't screaming the house down he was bashing his teeth out on the concrete floor. Little Jacob's extreme behaviour had taken its toll on his mum and dad, and

Nicky was on medication for depression. Their relationship was also at breaking point. There was something wrong with Jacob but no-one knew what it was.

Nicky was begging for help. She'd have walked over coals so that they could all be a family again. Although she had her doubts about psychics, she was desperate and willing to give anything a go.

A few minutes before I arrived I got myself into the zone. Almost instantly, I connected with the energy of a little boy. I noticed that he was desperate to communicate with me, so much so that he'd started before I'd even entered the building! I was standing on the path outside when I began to pick up feelings of anger and frustration from this child. There was definitely an extreme issue between the parents, and he wanted me to know as much about it as possible. This scared little boy was telling me that he was finding it hard to fit in with the rest of the family, and that this was really agitating him. He just seemed incredibly angry and frustrated. I knew I had a job on my hands here, and for an instant I was worried that I'd bitten off more than I could chew.

When I first introduced myself to Nicky and Stephen I was immediately told by Jacob to separate his mum and dad. So I asked Stephen to move to one end of the sofa and for mum to move to the other. I could feel Jacob's anger at this point, and the reading took a dramatic turn as soon as I let Jacob know I was ready to talk to him.

'Jacob's telling me that he likes to bang doors and turn light switches on and off,' I said. I was engulfed with the most powerful emotions while these images were being relayed to me. I started to cry and shake. I knew from my countless experiences with children that this was fairly unusual but I understood that Jacob was trying to tell me, in the best way he knew how, that he was sad and scared.

'He's telling me he is so angry and frustrated,' I said. 'He won't sleep and he doesn't care when you tell him when to go to sleep.' Inside me I could feel that this little boy would think nothing of going to bed whenever he wanted. The pain and anguish coming from him was really beginning to affect me and I burst into tears for a second time. Jacob was hurting badly. It would have been almost impossible for Jacob to continue the reading under such emotive circumstances as this would have exhausted both of us completely.

I looked at both Nicky and Stephen sitting on the sofa. I could sense that they knew exactly what I was talking about, even though we'd only just met. I asked Jacob to relax and he began to tell me about a particular book that he had, and how he liked to tear the pages out of it. So far, Nicky and Stephen were impressed by my accuracy.

Jacob was very keen to tell me about his mum. He showed me an image in my third eye of what I thought was a growth in her tummy. 'Have you been worried about a lump or ulcer?' I asked Nicky.

'No,' she replied. I went back to Jacob and asked him to confirm in more detail what he had just tried to tell me. He was quick to realize that I'd picked him up incorrectly so he gave me a full description of a baby in his mum's tummy.

'Okay, we are talking baby language here,' I said. 'Did you not think that you were pregnant Nicky?'

'Yes. I've been on medication for my depression and I missed four periods so I took a pregnancy test.' She seemed impressed by my comment. Then Jacob told me something that concerned me.

'I want you both to really listen to me. I'm not trying to scare you but it's important that he can't get near knives and forks. Jacob keeps telling me that it's very easy for him to get into the knife drawer.'

'He's always in the cutlery drawer, always,' said Nicky. 'How did you know that? How did you know?' She looked at Stephen and he looked back at her.

'Your son just told me. In case you didn't realize, I speak to children telepathically,' I joked. 'You've both been discussing moving, haven't you?'

'No,' said Nicky.

'Yes, you have. You've been on the phone, Nicky, talking to a friend about moving. Either she's moving or you are moving.' Jacob was telling me this information so I knew it was correct. Maybe Nicky was nervous under the spotlight or maybe she'd forgotten? Then, as if by magic, Nicky seemed to understand what I was talking about.

'Stephen and I are going through a bad patch at the moment so each of us has been considering moving out. I'd obviously been talking to my friend about this situation and that's where these details came from.' At that point Jacob stopped communicating with me. I had no idea why because it all seemed to be going well. Maybe I'd asked Jacob too many questions or perhaps we'd hit on something that was really affecting him. The initial reading was over so I'd have to leave that for next time.

Jacob was more than willing to talk to me when we got together later that week. 'Jacob tells me he has been very unsettled since the last time we met. You two have been at each other's throats over the past couple of days. He tells me that he has no guidelines as to when he is tired or when he feels that he wants to go to sleep.' I looked at both Nicky and Stephen as they sat together on their sofa. 'There are still a lot of emotions coming through from Jacob. He tells me that he also finds it very hard to show his love to you.' Nicky nodded, although Stephen made no attempt to acknowledge my remark. 'He does love you but there is a lack of knowledge about love and no discussions about love between you and Jacob. He's saying that you don't tell him you love him or care for him. It's a blank screen. It's this bond that we need to build upon to help him grow.'

I had their full attention by this point. Nicky went on to tell me that she also felt this way. 'I find it difficult to show my love to Jacob. I also have issues with Stephen and I'm unsure how I feel about him. I'm not sure if Stephen loves me either.' I could see that there were serious issues in this family. Maybe they were too much for me to sort out. Luckily, Jacob changed tack as if he knew he had to alter the tone of the reading.

'I'd like to talk to you both about sauces,' I said as I looked across at Nicky and Stephen. 'Just like the tomato sauces that go with beans or spaghetti. Have you not noticed that Jacob becomes very hyper when he eats these?' The family was listening but there was very little response. I then realized that I'd got the message slightly muddled and hadn't explained myself properly. 'I mean he gets hyper the next day. So if he ate some beans or spaghetti today, something with tomato sauce in it, then tomorrow he's crazy? You can't calm him down, no matter what you do.'

Nicky nodded. She knew exactly what I meant by this. Certain foods were causing problems for Jacob and we'd just got to the bottom of it. There were more messages coming through. One was very dark and it scared me. I had to tell Nicky and Stephen what it was. They had to know. 'I don't understand this. I'm just going to work through this. Is someone in prison or is someone going away to a building?' I tried to direct Jacob's message and asked him to tell me more. 'This is about a building and you going away to this building?' I looked at Nicky. She looked shocked and for a brief few moments lost her composure.

'Yes. I had a breakdown and ended up in hospital. No-one else knows about this, except the family.'

More information began to come through, and as I tuned in to Jacob I could feel his relief that I was suddenly sharing his hurt with his mum and dad. 'It's like being away and not being able to come out. It's like a prison,' I said. 'I can only gather from this that Jacob is still feeling part of the strain, the stress, the upset, the torment that you were and are still going through. It's hard for him to handle your depression and those feelings you are still – consciously or subconsciously – harbouring regarding your association with a mental institution. He's been constantly asking himself when this is going to get better.' Nicky started to get upset. 'This building has been horrific for him,' I added. 'He just doesn't understand what went on.' This was the last message I could get from

Jacob. I went back to him and concentrated but he didn't want to know. The reading was over, so I left Nicky and Stephen for a few minutes and went off to have a break. I was still thinking about what Jacob had just said but I didn't want to second-guess him. Hopefully, he would open up on my next visit.

I then put together a five point plan of action for the family to work through over the next seven days. I sat down on a chair directly opposite Stephen and Nicky. 'This five point plan isn't going to change your lives overnight but I hope we are going to take a step forward,' I said. 'The first issue is communication. Stop blaming each other. This lack of communication and your relationship breakdown is affecting your child. Look at how you are interacting, and how honest you are being with each other, especially regarding how you feel. Start to take some responsibility for your action and reactions.' By this point Nicky and Stephen were listening intently.

'The second issue is bedtimes. Jacob doesn't understand why people go to bed. You could consider talking to him about why it's important to go to sleep and why we sleep when it's dark outside.'

'We'll try that,' said Nicky, as she looked at Stephen. Stephen nodded back approvingly.

'The third issue is food. Jacob was telling me how certain foods make him hyper. Maybe you could evaluate what he is eating and possibly keep a note of how he behaves after eating these foods, hours or maybe days afterwards,' I suggested. By this time I was on a roll. 'The fourth issue is about expressing feelings; your feelings towards Jacob and your love for him. Maybe you could talk to Jacob about your childhoods and why you needed a mum and dad to help you? How it's important to have a mum and a dad in a family.' In my heart of hearts I wasn't sure how Stephen and Nicky were going to handle this issue, but life is full of surprises.

'The fifth and final issue is about the mental hospital,' I said. 'I know that it may be difficult but you should consider taking Jacob to the hospital one day. Maybe walk around the gardens if you can and let him know that people go there to heal, and to grow?' I looked at Nicky as I was talking this point through. I was hoping she was listening to me and not just hearing what I was saying. I really wanted this to work out for her, for the little boy who felt unloved and for her husband. 'Ultimately, it's up to you whether you act on the information but I wish you well with whatever you decide to do. I'm sure you'll make the best judgement for you and your family.'

When I returned a week later, Nicky and Stephen had a surprise in store for me. Things had improved. I decided to keep this meeting as informal as possible so we got together in the kitchen and had a chat over a cup of tea.

'The first thing I mentioned last week was communication, how you were relating to each other and your emotions towards Jacob and Sam. How's that been going?' Nicky looked embarrassed. 'Have you been cuddling each other?'

'No,' said Nicky. 'I'm sorry but I can't do that. We do hold a conversation. That's not too bad as we're not shouting and bawling at each other.' I could see from the look on Nicky's face that she found it awkward to talk about her feelings so I quickly moved on.

'How have you been coping with Jacob and Sam,' I asked.

'I've bonded so much more with Jacob now. We play together, we do everything together. I explain to him where I'm going, what I'm doing. When he's going to bed he doesn't have his tantrums anymore and he's not throwing his toys out of his room.'

'You'd shared with us that you'd had mental problems and been in a psychiatric ward. Did you go back with Jacob?' I asked Nicky.

'I have been back to the hospital with Jacob.'

'It must have been quite difficult for you.'

'It was very hard because it brought back a lot of bad memories.' I was so proud of Nicky for going through what must have been a harrowing experience.

'That was an amazing thing for you to do and you're a wonderful mum for putting yourself through that. I asked you to keep a note of what Jacob was eating. Have you done that?'

'Yes,' said Stephen. He pointed to the chart above my head. It was clear that Jacob's behaviour was linked to the tomato sauces we had discussed.

'All in all, has the last week been successful?'

'To me it has been really successful,' said Nicky. Stephen said nothing.

'I think what you've done has been fantastic. I'm looking forward to meeting Jacob now,' I replied.

It was time to sit with Jacob and find out what he thought. I took off my jacket and began to tune in to him telepathically. 'Hello, how are you?' I looked at Jacob and smiled. He was sitting on my chair, so I asked him verbally if I could sit down and he went off into the corner and started playing with one of his toys.

I connected with Jacob but he pulled away. I tried again to tune in but he pulled his energy away once more. I tried for a third time and he finally began to communicate with me. 'Jacob is showing me that he has a fear that everything will return to normal as soon as I am no longer involved with the family. He keeps showing me that he is scared that mum and dad will go back to their old ways.' The energy around these messages was very negative and black, as were the pictures Jacob was sending me. He was still a scared little boy so it didn't surprise me when he asked me to tell his mum to put his favourite toys out on display in his room.

'Would it be possible for you to put some of Jacob's toys out on display in his room, Nicky? Not too many, though. It's so he can look at these things. It gives him pleasure to look at cars or whatever.'

'Yes, of course I can do that.'

'Jacob is pleased things have changed but is worried that they might not continue. Is everything going to go topsy-turvy again? Are mum and dad really going to work at this?'

There are certain things I can help people with and certain things I cannot. I wondered how Nicky and Stephen would be able to set their differences aside for the sake of their son. With the meeting over I left the family for another week.

When I rang the doorbell seven days later, Jacob answered. I met with Stephen and Nicky in Jacob's bedroom. Stephen sat on the bed and Nicky sat on the floor with me. I could see that things weren't well in their relationship. Jacob seemed so much better but Stephen and Nicky didn't appear any more content than the first time I'd met with them. 'So, two weeks down the line, how are things?' I asked Nicky.

'I'm over the moon. I've got my son back and he's got his mum back.' I was interested to know how Nicky and Stephen's relationship was going. 'Have you managed to express your feelings towards each other?'

'Not really,' replied Nicky. 'Stephen does his thing and I do my thing.' I knew Nicky was telling the truth and I appreciated it.

'Do you think your relationship is something to work on then?' I asked.

'Yes, but I don't think it's going to happen overnight,' said Nicky.

'It's just going to take time,' said Stephen.

I was happy that I'd done the job I'd been asked to do. It was now up to Nicky and Stephen to sort out their side of the bargain.

I heard later that Stephen had been given an ultimatum by Nicky. He knew he had to change and get himself out of the big hole he was in or he could lose his wife and kids. I was also told that Stephen had taken the boys on holiday, which gave Nicky time to work out what her feelings really were for Stephen. She decided that she was going to be a mum and not a wife. Those days had gone and her future was with her children.

Madison's story – ruling the roost

Parents are always looking for tips on how to make family life happier and more fulfilling. Connecting with a child on a psychic level will help parents understand their baby's needs and wants to a much greater degree. Until now, parents may have thought that their baby could communicate only through crying, but I've seen that this is most definitely not the case.

How do our lives affect our babies? Are we being true to ourselves and our children? I believe that babies pick up on everything going on around them, even when they are asleep. They know all about your life. They can read your mind. They know when you are lying to them. They know when you hurt. They know when you are happy and when you are sad, and realize only too well when things are bothering you. When we are positive, our babies will feel it and thrive. When we are negative, our babies will pick up on that negativity and react to it in exactly the same fashion. That can mean tantrums, sleepless nights and the terrible twos.

What turns a toddler into a tyrant? Madison was just two years old and lived with her three-year-old sister, Alana, and her six-year-old brother, André, in Chesterfield. Although she was the youngest, she was constantly terrorizing the rest of the family by screaming all night long. In her house she was ruling the roost, especially at night.

For this little toddler every bedtime had become a battle, a battle her parents weren't winning. Madison's extreme behaviour was driving her parents apart and to despair. She had been known to wake up seven times in the night, and as mum, Nichola, had almost given up it was dad, Andrew, who'd usually be on night duty and it was exhausting him. Even if Nichola did get up during the night to help put Madison back to sleep, Madison would never go back down. She'd just scream all night long. Andrew was the only one who could put Madison back to bed, and he had to get up for work at six every morning.

Mum and dad had tried everything to help Madison. They'd been to the doctor and the health visitor, who'd both told them they were doing nothing wrong. Madison's parents were close to breaking point. Nichola and Andrew agreed to meet with me in a Manchester hotel. I had never met with them or spoken to them before our meeting.

I took a few moments to connect with Madison. She seemed a little unsure about speaking to me at first. I had to let her know that I was available to communicate with her. I was in the zone but she made it fairly obvious that she was the one in control.

When we did make contact, her first wish was that I separated her parents on the sofa. I therefore asked Andrew to sit to the left of me and Nichola to the right. It was then that Madison began to relax and spill the beans on her life. 'The first thing Madison is telling me is that the front door doesn't close properly and that there was a problem with that door when the family first moved into the house,' I said.

'That's correct,' said Nichola. 'We've been having a problem with the front door for quite some time.' Andrew smiled. I seemed to have hit the mark with my first comment. Surprisingly, Madison was fairly relaxed. I felt very comfortable speaking to her. It was as if for the first time she knew she could rely on someone. I tuned in to her and then she showed me a picture in my third eye of a key.

'Madison also tells me that Andrew had a problem getting a key cut and that the key wouldn't fit properly.'

'That's right,' replied Andrew. 'We've been having a problem with that lock.'

Madison then told me that she had a fear of being pushed out when mum and dad were together. 'She doesn't like it one bit when you are intimate with each other.'

'Andrew and I just can't get two minutes together. It's as if Madison hates it when I show any affection towards him. If we are having a hug she will come over and try to separate both of us.'

'Yes, that seems rather strange but I'm sure there is a reason for it. Give me a second and I'll ask Madison if she will tell us more about her feelings.' I had come out of the zone to speak with Nichola so I quickly reconnected with Madison, but unfortunately she wasn't prepared to give me any more details about her feelings towards her mum and dad. She then showed me an image of her trying to push her parents apart so that they slept in separate beds. 'She keeps mentioning to me about you being in separate beds and about bunk beds. There seems to be an issue with who sleeps in the bunk beds and how they sleep in them.'

'That's unbelievable,' said Nichola. 'Madison used to share bunk beds with her sister but they broke a while ago and they now share the unbroken bed, which we have in our own room. We've lost all our privacy since the girls moved in. I think that's what is causing some of the problems between Andrew and me.'

Madison was telling me many more things but they had to wait for our next meeting. I was fascinated by the family's sleeping arrangements. I was certain that this was one of Madison's main issues. I'd hit a nerve with Nichola and Andrew, but I knew there was a lot more work to do.

Afterwards I thought long and hard about Madison's reading. I hoped I hadn't been rude to the parents but I felt that their little girl was a control freak. I knew I'd have to visit the family on more than a few occasions just to appreciate how their child's mind worked. I just didn't understand why a two-year-old girl felt the need to control a family so much. I knew I needed to see the bigger picture. That was up to Madison, though. Would she let me into her world?

During the reading I noticed that Andrew had said he'd give his right arm for a good night's sleep. It wasn't hard to see that Andrew's chronic lack of sleep had been affecting not only him but also the rest of the family. He just didn't seem to have any time to sort himself out, or anything else for that matter. Even though I hadn't yet been to visit the family home, I'd got the distinct impression from Madison that there was stuff everywhere and that their house was a mess. Maybe I should have mentioned this during the reading but I didn't want to embarrass her mum and dad.

I was looking forward to meeting the family again. As I approached the house I was conscious about getting myself into the zone. I felt that I needed Madison to know I was coming and that I was a friend, not a foe. Nichola and Andrew were waiting for me when I arrived and they seemed pleased to see me. Madison was also there and didn't bother with me, but that wasn't so unusual. Some children have a tendency to ignore me when I first arrive at their home. It seems to be their way of letting me know that they are in control of the situation and that I am a guest in their environment.

'Hello, how are you? I see that you have some cats,' I said. 'How are you, Madison?' Madison continued to play at her parents' feet, pretending to ignore me as Nichola and Andrew sat pensively on the sofa, waiting to hear what I had to say. The first message that came through from Madison was about balloons. She kept showing me balloons in my third eye and then that she was unhappy when she was with the balloons. I felt a surge of energy within me and could feel she was trying to tell me that she'd had a tantrum when she'd been at a party or some event that had balloons. 'I'm feeling a bit of a tantrum coming on,' I said to Nichola and Andrew. 'Madison keeps showing me balloons and telling me that she was at a party or at McDonald's recently. She's just told me that she got juice but no food. Remember when you went home that night after that party?'

'Yes, I remember it well,' said Nichola. She smiled at Andrew, but he didn't smile back. Obviously, Nichola knew something Andrew didn't.

'Madison is telling me that she acted up because a drink made her hyper. Can you confirm that it was either a red or orange drink that caused Madison to act up, Nichola?'

'Yes. It was a red drink. I remember coming home from that party and giving Madison that juice. She loves it, it's her favourite.'

I was prepared to do anything I could to help Madison so I couldn't hold back, no matter how awful I might feel afterwards. 'I've got to tell you this but I need to be very honest. Madison's finding it very difficult to understand why things are not in their place and kept in their place.' Nichola laughed. The house was an utter mess. It was the untidiest house I had ever been in. Madison seemed to be crying out for someone to help her mum and dad get their lives in order. 'Madison has just told me that she can't find the videos because they've been moved,' I added. Yet again, Nichola laughed and I noticed that Andrew now had a smirk on his face. I was surprised. In a roundabout way they knew what I was talking about yet didn't seem embarrassed. A stranger was commenting on the way they lived but they weren't in the least bit bothered. But Madison had more to say so the reading went off in another direction.

'Madison is now telling me about a bulb getting changed in a bedroom. Do you understand that Andrew?'

'Yes.'

'She's upset with you, Andrew, because you took longer than you should have to change the bulb.'

Everyone laughed.

'Because, yet again, you made excuses about it, Andrew, didn't you?'

'I always do,' said Andrew. He squirmed in his chair and crossed his legs. I had hit a nerve.

'It's these excuses that infuriate Madison. She's saying to me that she can't understand how mum and dad can put themselves on a pedestal when they don't practise what they preach.'

'Go girl,' said Nichola, laughing, but this wasn't funny. Her daughter was in trauma and hurting inside. She needed mum and dad to listen and not to patronize her.

'Madison tells me that there was something about water coming in through the roof. She's also telling me that you were stupid to let the water come in.'

'It's not our fault,' said Andrew. 'We had a problem with a leak some months ago and the council still haven't come to fix it. We weren't stupid and let the water come in; that's not the way it happened.'

'But if it was Madison who'd made a mess you'd be telling her immediately to go and clean it up or fix it. But if it's between you two, the parents, well you seem to just meander about. You're not bothered, or you just wait to see what will happen and maybe you'll do something about it at some point. But when will that be? There is dishonesty in this house that STINKS!' There was silence. I thought someone was going to get up and punch me, but thankfully I had at least six members of the production crew to help me out if things got messy!

Yet again, Madison changed the subject very quickly. I found this rather strange and contradictory. I could feel Madison was pleading for help yet I could sense that she didn't like confrontations. 'Madison has no frame of reference about when is the right time to go to sleep. This causes you both problems when you also want to go to bed.'

'I'm always totally exhausted so Madison is right to tell you that,' said Nichola. 'That's why the house is such a mess. I just can't seem to get anything done. I'm tired all the time.'

'I feel that you have both just capitulated. You're holding up the white flag and saying, "Madison, we give in!" By giving in you have let your daughter know that the way she is acting is okay.' I could sense from Madison at this point that I was saying all the things she wanted me to say. 'I don't want to appear rude but you have been very weak.' Both Nichola and Andrew looked at me and seemed surprised, but I knew deep down that they understood exactly why I was saying it. 'Do you really love your daughter? Because all I'm feeling here is Madison getting really angry with you. She feels she's talking to a brick wall. She feels that when I go away nothing will change because mum's just going to sit and smile and laugh about it all. But Madison wants to know if mummy is really going to pick up on what she needs.' Nichola looked at me and began to nod. 'Is dad going to pick up on it?' I continued. 'Is dad going to do anything about how Madison feels because Madison is very angry! The reason she's angry is because she feels she is not growing and getting what she needs out of life, and you are her only support network.'

I knew from the look they both gave me that Andrew and Nichola realized the truth only too well. 'I can sit with her all day and tell you what Madison is thinking but unless you are going to get up off your backsides and do something about it you'll be in the same situation for years.'

I decided to take a break from the reading and leave the family to think through what had just happened. I felt slightly embarrassed for Nichola and Andrew. I knew they were good, honest, hard-working people whom you'd be pleased to call friends. It must have been hard for them to be taken to task quite brutally by their own two-year-old.

Their daughter loved them – that was obvious – but she was feeling very frustrated, hurt and upset, and it was my job to let her parents know how she felt.

I put a three point plan together to set down in black and white what I'd been told by Madison during the reading. This was designed to stimulate Andrew and Nichola into changing certain aspects of their lives in order to solve Madison's issues. I was confident that once these issues were resolved, Madison's problems would no longer exist and she would become the normal, happy child her mum and dad so wanted. I returned 20 minutes later.

'Thank you very much for allowing me to come and see you today. I really appreciate it. I know it's been a very difficult reading but I'd really like to address a few points that Madison brought up.' Nichola and Andrew were shell-shocked and dazed, but maybe this was the wake-up call they needed. 'The first point is about structure,' I said. 'Madison doesn't know when she should go to sleep or why she should go to sleep. So maybe you'd like to consider thinking about bedtimes, and what you say to Madison before she goes to bed.' I noticed Nichola nod approvingly.

'Madison said a few times that you make excuses and put things off. Maybe you'll start cleaning the floor and stop halfway through. She finds this very hard to address and understand. The second point, therefore, is about tidying up. There's a place for everything and everything should be in its place. If you don't respect things then how can your daughter respect you?' I hoped that Nichola and Andrew were listening to this point as it seemed so critical to Madison's reading.

'The third point is about the red or orange drink. Madison tells me that she gets very hyper after drinking this. So possibly it's time to reassess the drink Madison is having. Ultimately, though, it's up to you, but I wish you every success and hope you've enjoyed your reading.' I kissed Nichola and gave Andrew a hug. I think they both needed it. I certainly did!

When I returned a week later I could see immediately that the family had been busy as there was a half-full skip in the drive. I was concerned, though, that they might have given up halfway through. That skip should have been full. They'd been given a week to get the house tidy and they knew I was coming back, but I was willing to give them the benefit of the doubt!

Nichola and Andrew actually looked pleased to see me, which was a bit of a surprise after the bombardment of abuse they'd received a week earlier. They were busy in their lounge, putting countless belongings into 30 or so cardboard boxes. My goodness, they had a lot of junk in their house! It was all going into storage.

'So what have you got out of the last week?' I asked. 'Have things changed for you and Madison?'

'She's not getting up as many times,' replied Nichola.

'I've noticed a lot of change,' said Andrew. 'Especially in the amount of times Madison gets out of bed during the night.'

'Remind me,' I added. 'How many times was she normally getting up during the night?'

'Anything between three and seven,' replied Nichola.

'What's it down to now?

'It's about two to three times,' replied Andrew.

'Well, that's a great improvement, an amazing change.' I was happy to hear this.

'It has been great for me,' added Andrew. Both Nichola and Andrew seemed to be pleased that the changes were resulting in real improvements with Madison's night-time behaviour. This was all very well but I decided to talk to Madison. I wanted to know how she felt about the changes her mum and dad were making. I was concerned that this was just a flash in the pan and that things might return to normal once the honeymoon period was over.

Madison was really happy about talking to me and immediately confirmed my fears. She told me she was scared that her parents would give up again once the cameras had gone. There was more to come and I knew Nichola wouldn't like what I was about to say. 'Madison's conscious of you and your thoughts, especially those thoughts about your weight. She tells me she doesn't want to be fat like her mum, because she knows that being fat makes you feel insecure.'

Nichola was shocked. 'I feel bad enough about my weight without my kids being affected by it.' She was sobbing.

'Have you been thinking very negatively about your body?'

'Yes, and I keep thinking I want to do something about it.'

'Maybe now is the time to make inroads into changing your life.'

I felt sorry for Nichola. I knew deep down that she was a really nice person and I felt awful that she was being given such a mauling by her own daughter. But maybe she needed to hear some home truths. Perhaps by doing what she was doing, the way she was doing it, Madison knew this was the only way her mother would change. 'Have you noticed that when Madison gets bored she wants to eat?' I asked.

'Yes,' replied Nichola.

'We need to try and watch that,' I added. Then Madison flashed the most unlikely picture into my third eye. 'I've just been shown grapes. I think Madison wants you to put out a bowl of grapes and juice for her. Buy some healthy foods she can snack on when she feels the need.'

The meeting had come to an emotional end. I knew Nichola would be more demoralized than Andrew, but maybe this was her time to think about the way she was living her life. This could be her light bulb moment. I wasn't so sure though.

I decided to approach my final meeting with Nichola and Andrew carefully as I didn't want to upset anyone. 'What I'd really like to do, guys, is just go through what's been happening over the past few weeks. Tidying up was one of the main issues that came up. Have you got to the stage where you are happy with the tidying?' The house was still a total mess.

'There is still more to do,' said Andrew. 'We've found the last week really tiring.'

'We've felt under a hell of a lot of pressure,' said Nichola. 'It's caused friction.'

'Ultimately there are pressures here because you want to help your daughter,' I said. 'So it's Catch-22.'

'Yesterday someone asked me how I felt about what we've achieved,' said Nichola. 'I said I didn't feel we'd achieved anything.'

'Were you doing it for you, Nichola,' I asked. 'Or were you doing it for your daughter?' Nichola was beginning to sound like a spoilt child and I felt I had to remind her that she was in fact a wife and mother with three children.

'No, I'm doing it for Madison,' said Nichola.

'What I'm getting here is, "Oh, hasn't this been really bad for me". Let's put your hand on your heart here. Do you think you've put enough effort in?'

'I think more could have been done if I'd not been at work,' said Andrew.

'I've done as much as I've felt able to do,' said Nichola.

'Well, that's not really an answer,' I added.

'I've had the kids and I've been on my own during the day. There is only so much you can do when you have kids running round you because as fast as you are doing one thing they are destroying something else.'

'Look, you are a team. There are two adults here. I don't have children, so shoot me down, but surely one adult can look after the children. There are one-parent families in Britain. Some of these parents have more than three kids and they cope. Would this not leave one of you free?' Nichola and Andrew started to argue. I'd had enough and was ready to let rip. 'Look, I came to see you guys, and one of the things your daughter told me was that she wanted the house tidied. Okay? That was the whole point of doing this.'

'But we're trying,' added Andrew.

I couldn't believe what I was hearing. It seemed to be one excuse after another, and exactly what Madison had been dreading. 'Look, I think you are just making excuses. The house is still messy!'

'This is us!' exclaimed Nichola.

'But your daughter doesn't want it to be like this!'

'There has been an improvement,' insisted Nichola.

'But it's not enough!' I exclaimed.

'I'm not sitting here, listening to this,' protested Nichola. 'I'm sorry, Derek, but I'm finding this very offensive. Could you cut the cameras please?' Nichola got up from the sofa. I wanted to continue the discussion but it was no good. Nichola was in tears. 'Look, Derek, I need 10 minutes,' she added, picking up Madison and storming off.

'Nichola, if this is the way you react then no wonder your daughter is in the state she's in. This is all about you, you, you Nichola, and not about your daughter.'

I had to say what I'd just said. Madison needed her mum to hear this and hear it well. I'd been giving Nichola and Andrew the benefit of the doubt for too long. They honestly needed a good kick up the backside. Nichola was in tears, and as Andrew walked by me to go and see her I flinched. I honestly thought he was going to hit me!

I'd never come across people like Nichola and Andrew before. I think that they were so stuck in their comfort zones that no-one could get through to them easily. Maybe I had achieved something though. We would all have to wait and see.

I didn't see Nichola and Andrew again. In fact, I didn't hear anything about their progress until I was invited to see a preview of their show. I couldn't believe the changes they'd made since I'd left. Madison had a gorgeous bedroom and the house looked tidy. Nichola and Andrew looked well too, and it was great to hear that Madison now slept during the night. Nichola was interviewed at the end of the show and explained how Madison was now a different little girl. Madison didn't have half as many tantrums as before. Although she usually got up once a night, that was to get a drink and then — surprise, surprise — she would go back to sleep! Nichola was now conscious that she was a mum who needed to provide for her children in a way she'd never thought about before. She had started to consider what her children needed rather than what she thought they needed. There was much more fruit and healthier things to eat in the house, and the red drink was a thing of the past.

Nichola and Andrew's relationship had also improved greatly, and Madison wasn't splitting them up anymore. They now had more privacy in their own bedroom. It was good to see that they were also working more as a team. They seemed much more at ease and contented, and said they had actually enjoyed their experience with me. Maybe I did something right after all!

Teagan's story –
out of control

I've spent a great deal of time with mums and dads over the years, and I've noticed that creating a beautiful son or daughter doesn't suddenly make them able parents. Past experiences and current state of mind can really affect children, even when these feelings are at an unconscious level. I've become aware that babies and young children can recognize traumas that occurred in their parents' lives even before they were born.

These fundamentals must be recognized before parents can move forward. In essence, if we want our children to behave 'better', we have to be prepared to examine our own behaviour more thoroughly. Only then can we begin the process of understanding our children more deeply.

I'd love to be perfect. I have troubles like everyone else. I get angry. I get frustrated. I get stressed and yet I realize that I have to put these troubles to one side when I need to connect with children telepathically. I have learnt to put things in perspective and never to allow negative thoughts to take over my life.

Teagan was completely out of control. The toddler screamed without letting up, was continually violent and woke throughout the night. Single mum Emma had to handle this wild behaviour all on her own. Teagan would bite Emma, pinch and kick her and pull her hair. It got to the point where Emma dreaded waking up each morning because she knew what would greet her.

Emma had taken Teagan to the doctor and he had prescribed sedatives but even these hadn't worked. It was getting too much and Emma was finding it very difficult to cope. Was there something wrong with Teagan? The pressure on Emma had been so unbearable that she'd even considered giving Teagan up to social services. Emma took large quantities of caffeine tablets to get through each day. Was I to be Emma's glimmer of hope? I had two weeks to turn her life around, and I knew from the minute I laid my eyes on Teagan that this would be one of my biggest challenges yet.

I met with Emma and Teagan in London at a neutral location. We had never spoken before or had any contact. I started to connect with Teagan before I got to the location. This wasn't so strange as it had happened to me before. It was a good sign though. It meant that the child was in the correct frame of mind to communicate with me. She began to tell me that she had a very low attention span and a major issue with her mother. The child was in my zone so I was looking forward to the first brief 15-minute reading.

When I arrived, I sat down on the floor beside the sofa where Emma and Teagan were sitting. I asked Emma to be as relaxed with me as she could. I also asked her to let Teagan sit on the floor because I could feel their bond was very close. When this is the case it's sometimes difficult for the energy from the child to flow directly to me because the mother can unwittingly block that energy path with her subconscious thoughts.

'I'm going to talk about personal things. Is that okay?' I asked Emma. Emma agreed so I started the reading. I was nervous because I knew in my heart of hearts where it was going to lead, but I was hoping that other information would come through. 'Teagan tells me that you have some issue with your feet. I think it's to do with the fact that you don't like to show your feet or wear open-toed sandals.'

'Yes,' said Emma. She seemed confused.

'Before you came today, or possibly last night, you were suffering from stomach cramps,' I added.

'Yes,' Emma laughed nervously. I'd struck a chord with her.

'I don't want to be rude here but Teagan's got a very low attention span. She's telling me that you don't treat her like a daughter, that you are more like sisters. You find it very hard to control her.' I could feel Teagan's imagery in my third eye at this point and it was very strong. She was showing me how difficult it was for her when she was out shopping with her mum. 'You get nervous about telling her off. You don't know where the boundaries are with Teagan and she doesn't know where they are with you.' I added.

Teagan started to get annoyed at this moment. I could sense mixed emotions flowing through my body. It was like panic was about to set in. Teagan was obviously finding it difficult to control her feelings.

'I want to scream,' I said. Emma looked shocked. I continued talking. 'I don't want to scare you here, Emma, but Teagan is telling me to let you know how she feels and this is the best way for me to show you.' It was all getting a bit strange now. I could see Emma squirming in her seat. 'Teagan wants to scream the house down when she does-n't get her own way,' I added. I could feel this incredible energy all over my body. It was powerful stuff. 'Have I got your attention now, Emma?'

'Yes.'

'Am I scaring you?'

'Yes.' Emma looked flustered. She probably had no idea what I was going to say next.

'Good.' I needed Emma to be aware at this point that Teagan was talking to me and telling me her feelings. 'The major issue in your life, Emma, is your insecurity, full stop. You keep questioning everything you do. That's being reflected onto your daughter, and that's why she's acting the way she is. She's feeling what you are feeling.'

Emma broke down. She was in floods of tears so I comforted her. I then saw some horrendous imagery in my third eye. I was shocked but not surprised. I knew something was upsetting Teagan and it had to be something big. 'You've also got secrets you've kept from your family regarding sexual situations in your life, and your daughter knows about them.' I knew at that very moment what these issues were, as Teagan had just shown me, but now wasn't the time to go into that area of Emma's life. I had to be sensitive and respect her privacy, at least until I was with her in her own home. I had to be careful about her emotional state on the journey home. Too much information at once can be dangerous so it was time to call it a day. Emma seemed convinced by my abilities and I knew she wanted help from me. I was looking forward to seeing her again in her own home.

Emma lived in Southend. I'd never been there before so I was looking forward to going for a walk on the beach. I was slightly taken aback when we turned up at her home to start filming. Emma lived on the 11th floor of a tower block, and I don't like heights! I kept well back from the windows and didn't look out. I knew if I did I'd have to get out of there very quickly before I started screaming the place down. If it had been a contest between Teagan and me I know who would have won!

When I stepped out of the lift I felt that Teagan knew I was there. There were a few messages coming through at that point but I knew they would get stronger when I entered their apartment. Teagan was waiting for me and we connected when I walked into their lounge. 'Teagan is telling me that your tummy has been sore again, Emma,' I said. 'Your tummy's been unsettled for the past few days.'

Emma nodded. 'I'm having my period.' Emma didn't seem as perky as she had been in London. Maybe I had scared her. I decided to take things easy, if Teagan would let me. It isn't unusual for children to tell me about their own or other people's state of health when I first start to tune in.

'Teagan's also telling me that she has a birthmark on her bum. It's on her left buttock.'

'Yes.' Emma looked shocked.

'She's telling me just now …' I couldn't finish my sentence. I felt a huge rush of information to my head and it was overwhelming. 'Oh, oh,' I said. 'Please take it one step at a time, Teagan.'

Emma looked at me as if I was nuts, but I was trying to calm Teagan down. She wanted to tell me too much at once. I think she'd just realized that I was her voice. 'She's telling me that she likes jumping on the bed like a trampoline. She wants a trampoline. We have to get Teagan a trampoline. She's also telling me that she loves to dress up. She wants to dress up as a fairy or a princess but she wants to do it properly. She wants to start at the beginning and see it through to the end. You have a tendency to start and not finish, Emma, okay?'

'Yes.'

'Teagan is telling me that she finds it very uncomfortable to be in her room. She doesn't like being on her own when she's to go to sleep. She's telling me that she's very clingy and that she wants you to be with her. Sometimes she won't sleep even when you are with her.'

'That makes sense,' replied Emma. Teagan then showed me a picture in my third eye of her getting ready for bed and her mum giving her sweets to keep her quiet. These sweets weren't doing her any good at all.

'Have you been giving her sweeties before she goes to bed?'

Emma laughed. 'Some nights I do.'

'It has to stop. It's making her hyperactive.'

'Yes. I've noticed that she's been acting up when I put her down at night. I had no idea the sweets were doing it though.' I knew I'd struck another chord with her, and I didn't want to lose her concentration.

'Stay with me Emma, stay with me. This is Teagan's time to talk to her mummy.' I knew that now was the time to talk about something that had really been bothering Teagan. This was what I'd kept back from our first meeting but Teagan was showing me those pictures again. I would have to tread carefully so I started slowly. 'I want to talk about dreams, Emma. Can we talk about dreams?'

'Yes, you can.'

'Can we talk about scary dreams? Can we talk about nightmares?'

'Yes,' replied Emma, sheepishly.

'Can we talk about nightmares about being 14?' There was silence. Emma was becoming slightly alarmed but I had to continue. 'Teagan knows that you have nightmares about being 14 and a man coming to get you.'

'Yes,' said Emma. I could see her shaking.

'It's horrible,' I said. I hid my head in my hands. I was seeing exactly what had happened to Emma and it was distressing me. I was also concerned about Teagan because she was the one sending me this information. It was all so very worrying. 'This is really freaking Teagan out,' I said. 'Right, we need to work through this. This is a time in your life that Teagan has found really difficult to handle. What I'm being shown by Teagan is a situation when you had sex with someone you didn't want to have sex with. I'm going to use the word "rape" if I can.'

'Yes.'

'This has left a huge mark on you, a big black cloud and an incredible weight on your shoulders, and on your baby's shoulders. The rape has stopped you from moving forward and has made you feel dirty about yourself and your sexuality. It has also made you lock yourself away.' Emma was in floods of tears but I had to continue. 'This is really affecting your child.' I picked up some tissues and gave Emma a hug. 'Emma, I just had to bring this up because it's very important that you deal with this to help you and your child.' I composed myself because I knew what I was about to say was going to upset Emma even more. 'Another reason why Teagan isn't sleeping well is because she is scared that when she becomes 14, 15 or 16 that some bad man will come and rape her because it happened to her mum.'

'I didn't want her to know all that. I don't want her living in my past.' I cuddled Emma. At this difficult time she needed to know that there were people around her who cared.

I left Emma to gather her thoughts. This was an area outside my expertise so I had to tread carefully. I understood that Emma was now happy because she'd been told what Teagan's main problem was. I could sense that she felt excited about the future and that her life was about to change. She'd found out why things had been going wrong all this time. Emma knew if she sorted herself out then Teagan would be sorted too.

I put together a plan of action in order to help Teagan. I was going to leave this plan with Emma, and it was up to her whether she followed it or not. 'I've put together a plan for you to consider, Emma. The first thing is about addressing your past. The biggest issue that came out of your reading was the rape. Maybe you could consider speaking to a psychologist or someone who knows what to say and how to guide you.' Emma listened intently. I could see for the first time that she was crying out for help.

'The next point is about positive attitude. Teagan seems to get very frustrated when her mum is not in control, when her mum's depressed. She was telling me that she doesn't sleep well when you have a down day. Maybe you could think about being more positive?'

'Okay.' Emma could hear me but I didn't think she was really listening. I knew there were many things going on in her mind. I was glad I'd written down those points so she could have a look at them later when she'd got over her rollercoaster reading.

'The next point is about diet. Teagan told me that sweets were making her hyperactive.'

'Will I give her a carrot instead?' joked Emma.

'Well, you could if you wanted to. Maybe give her a balanced diet using more natural foods.'

'I'll try that.'

'The next two points are really about Teagan. She told me that she wanted a trampoline. She also mentioned that she loves glitter and dressing up because she wants to be a child, so tomorrow perhaps you could think about buying her a trampoline and getting her some dressing-up clothes, maybe a princess dress or a fairy costume? Ultimately, though, this reading is about being positive, dealing with the past, looking forward to the future and letting your daughter know that her mummy's in control.'

'Thank you,' said Emma. 'You've been amazing. Thank you so much for coming to see Teagan today.' We hugged and I left.

It was all over. A difficult reading had hopefully opened the door to a wonderful future for both Teagan and her mum. I was looking forward to seeing them in a week's time.

Emma seemed pleased to see me when I walked into her lounge. 'Hello,' I said, 'A new face!'

'This is my mum.'

I asked Emma how things were going.

'Yeah, they are going really well. Teagan's sleeping all night now.' Teagan started laughing and I took that opportunity to ask her to connect telepathically with me and tell me what had been going on since I'd last seen the family.

'Listen, the atmosphere in this house has completely changed,' I said.

'Do you think so?'

'Yes. But I've got to say that you're not quite there yet.'

'Not quite. I thought that myself.' Some more information started to come through from Teagan.

'You are still getting negative feelings. You still have those haunting, negative feelings.' Teagan then asked me to tell Emma a few things. 'Teagan can't change what's in your head. You have to work on that. Now I left you with the plan and in it I said that maybe you could speak to someone about your past.'

'I'm going this week,' said Emma.

'Fantastic! Teagan's telling me that even though she's been great she's been having the odd tantrum.'

'Yes.'

'She's fine then suddenly there's a tantrum, and you're like, where did that come from?' Emma smiled and nodded. I looked over at Teagan and pointed. 'That's her getting frustrated at you for not dealing with what's in your head. She wants to send you lots of love and she's saying to me, "but mum's really trying".'

'Yes.'

'So a couple of tantrums a day, which will go.'

'Hopefully they will.' Emma didn't seem very confident.

'But even by saying "hopefully" you are being negative, Emma. Teagan is picking that up. STOP BEING NEGATIVE. BE A POSITIVE MUM.'

Emma started to laugh. I knew I couldn't be any more forceful. It was up to her if she wanted to help her child. She just had to stay positive and stop giving out all her negative crap to Teagan.

'Now, did you get her the trampoline?' I asked.

'Well, I tried. I need to ask you about that actually. I took her into the shop expecting her to love this trampoline.' I immediately got a message from Teagan telling me that she'd had a tantrum in the shop because her mum wasn't happy about being there with her.

'Did she not have a bit of a tantrum when you were in the shop?'

'A massive one. I tried to put the fairy dress on her and she didn't want it.'

Some more messages started to come through from Teagan. I knew exactly what to say. 'I get a mum, in a shop, panicking. "Who's looking at me? Oh my God!" That's all going on in your head, isn't it?'

'Yes,' replied a rather stunned Emma.

'Right. Teagan is picking up on this. If she sees you panicking it affects her and then she starts to react. If you'd bought the trampoline and brought it back here she would have loved it.' I now had Emma's attention. 'So go and get it tomorrow.'

Emma started laughing. I wasn't sure if this was nervous laughter or just relief. I now turned my attention to Emma's mum, Wendy. There were a few things I wanted to mention to her, and I got the impression that she was a sceptic. 'So how come I've got the privilege of meeting you today?'

'I've come to check you out.'

'What do I need to do to impress you?' I asked with a smile. I knew what I was going to say though. Teagan had told me a few things about Wendy already, but there was also a spirit in the room who began to talk to me. 'Let's talk about smell. Teagan is talking to me just now and she's telling me that her socks are smelly. Do you understand that, Wendy?'

'I took her socks off just before you came in, Derek, and put them to my nose and told Teagan that they stank,' replied a startled Wendy.

Teagan started to tell me more about Wendy. 'I'm going to say something that may shock you. Can I continue?'

'Yes, that's fine.'

'Can you validate a miscarriage?'

'Yes.'

'You lost a son.' Wendy burst into tears and I suddenly felt very sorry for her. Teagan knew her secret too. I could sense the spirit of Wendy's son standing just by the door as I told Wendy more about him. 'Did you know that you'd lost a boy?'

'Yes, I did, Derek.' I felt I now had to tell Wendy where I was getting this information from. 'Now the weird thing is that Teagan knows about this. This has been going on a lot in your head, hasn't it?' Wendy was crying her eyes out. 'You've been having thoughts about this loss and how you've dealt with it. That was a very difficult time for you. Do you want me to continue?'

'On you go.' I sat down beside Wendy on the sofa and put my arm around her. 'Do you remember at the time of your miscarriage there was an alcohol problem going on, some sort of drink problem?'

'There was afterwards.'

'Yes. Teagan's showing me lots of booze and drink and a feeling of not being able to cope. She wants to give you big hugs and to tell you that she loves you very much. That's one of the reasons why she behaves so well with you. She knows what you've been through. She knows that you try and make up now for the hurt you've had in the past. Do you completely understand this?'

'Yes.'

It was time to get out of there. I needed some air and to allow Emma and her mum to come to terms with what I'd just said. I was sure that Wendy now believed in me. Having spent time with Emma and Wendy, I'd picked up on their difficult relationship. Emma had to feel that she could go to her mum, and Wendy had to make herself approachable.

I put a new plan together and went back into the lounge. 'Your mum is a tremendous support. You've probably not noticed that yet. Having said that, Wendy, you have to give Emma the confidence to approach you, and let her know that you will help her with any problems.'

'I always tell my kids that anyway,' said Wendy.

'But it doesn't seem to be working that well. You might be there for Emma but maybe Emma's a bit unsure whether she wants to accept that help or not. Now this is all about Teagan and making her happy, but you all have to work at this. There's no point in doing something if you're not pulling together as a team.' I said my goodbyes and gave Emma and Wendy a big hug. I looked forward to seeing everyone the following week.

So it was D-day. When I walked into Emma's flat I was surprised that her mum, Wendy, wasn't there. Emma seemed happy to see me, though, and she looked well. Teagan was playing happily in her bedroom, so I had a few moments to speak to Emma without any interruptions. 'Tell me, how are things?' I asked, hoping that everything was good.

'There has been a massive improvement,' said Emma. 'Teagan has completely changed. She is really, really happy now. She's sleeping all night and having hardly any tantrums. It's weird but she's all cute and cuddly. She was nothing like that two weeks ago. I just like spending time with her now. I also feel more of a mum. I don't feel like a bad mum at all.'

I was really happy to hear this news. 'So did you get Teagan the party dress and the trampoline?'

'Yes, I did. I went to the shop as you said and brought them both back home, and she absolutely loved them. She acted so differently from the little girl who had the tantrum in the shop. She always wears her fairy dress and loves playing on her trampoline. She is such a happy, contented little girl now.'

'How do you see your relationship with Teagan growing?'

'Well, two weeks ago I couldn't even look forward to the next day, let alone a whole future. Now I'm really looking forward to it because I have her back and she's all happy again.'

Emma had also started seeing a psychologist. I was happy to hear she'd taken that first step. I was still anxious, though, to find out if Emma and her mum were beginning to provide one another with emotional support. 'How has your relationship with your mum progressed?'

'That's one of the things we've got to do slowly, I think. It's not going to happen just like that. I actually told my mum that I loved her the other night. I've never done that before and then I started to cry!'

'So exciting times ahead?'

'Very exciting times I hope.'

It was all over. The job had been a hard one but I'd done what I'd set out to do. I'd changed two lives, and hopefully more. I now realized why Emma had applied to be on the show. She was a beautiful young woman who'd been hurt at a young age and was crying out for help. Now she could go on without fearing that her child would hurt or embarrass her, and for that I'm thankful to God for my gift and for blessing me with the ability to make dreams come true.

Lilly's story – the baby who hit her mother

I've discovered over time that children will tell me their innermost worries and fears if they trust me and the conditions are right. Children tell me the way it is, the truth. There are no lies and no nonsense. When I communicate with them they usually get to the point very quickly and let me know what's troubling them. Maybe their parents' relationship is upsetting them, and that's why they are restless at night. Perhaps they're not very happy about the colour of their bedroom, which is why they won't sleep until they're tucked up with mum in her room. Or maybe they are allergic to certain foods, which are making them hyperactive and upsetting their tummy. Even the way a parent drives their car can affect children in the strangest ways. Parents should also realize that the most flippant comment can disturb their child. There will be a reason for everything a child does. You just have to find out what it is!

Gemma lived in Chatham with her 21-month-old daughter, Lilly, and Lilly was out of control. Her daily screaming fits had taken over the life of single mum Gemma. When Lilly went outside, the tantrums just got worse. If that wasn't bad enough, Lilly had started attacking Gemma. She would punch, head-butt and bite her. The stress of coping alone was proving too much for Gemma. Something was troubling Lilly but Gemma couldn't understand the cause of her violent behaviour. I was given two weeks to transform Lilly from a violent child into a loving daughter.

Every day, Gemma had to sit with Lilly and feed her with a spoon like a baby. The real problems occurred when Gemma tried to get Lilly ready to go out. This could take Gemma nearly an hour. Lilly would scream and shout, which made Gemma feel a failure as a mum, but when the screaming and shouting stopped the violent behaviour started. It was easier for Gemma to stay in with Lilly and watch cartoons than to go through these daily fights. When Gemma did manage to leave the house, Lilly would kick and scream until they got home. The strain of looking after Lilly was taking its toll. Sceptical Gemma decided to meet me at a neutral location in London.

I was looking forward to my new challenge. As always, I'd been given no information about the family before meeting them. I began to tune in to Lilly as soon as I entered the room. She immediately pulled back, though, the minute we looked at each other. I introduced myself to Gemma and Lilly and sat directly across from Gemma as Lilly played around on the floor. For the first 10 minutes or so, Lilly blocked me. I could feel a huge amount of hurt engulfing my body but that was about it. The hurt was so strong that I had to fight back the tears. Then some information started to come through. It was all very sporadic.

'Lilly's telling me that she loves to go up and down stairs.'

'Yes, that's right.'

'Someone's been cutting a hedge, just outside this particular house where there are also stairs.' This was my way of validating to Gemma that Lilly was connecting with me.

'Yes,' said Gemma. She didn't seem very impressed though. Suddenly, Lilly decided to tell me some personal details about her life.

'The problem with you, Gemma, is that you're not spending enough time looking after yourself. There is too much time with Lilly. For you to grow you have to get out of the looking-after-Lilly mode because it is suffocating your daughter.' I looked over at Gemma and she broke down. I had to continue. 'I want you to stay with me, Gemma, because Lilly wants you to know these things.' I got the impression that I was losing Gemma and that her emotions were getting the better of her. 'You have a problem when you go outside. You change. You feel that people are looking at you. You feel that people are looking at Lilly. You also feel that people are judging you. Lilly is telling me that this is going on in your head. Do you understand this?'

'Yes.' I decided not to continue with this part of the reading as I didn't want to say too much about this particular problem at our first meeting. I asked Lilly if she would move on and tell me something else about her life.

Lilly then showed me a plate with a knife, fork and spoon. I realized there was negative energy around the image and understood what she was trying to say to me. 'I want to talk about food, okay?'

'Yes.'

'Now, Lilly's at the stage where she's almost scared to use a fork instead of a spoon. You've noticed this, haven't you?'

'Yes.' Gemma's face went slightly red. I knew I had just hit on something that was really bothering her.

'Lilly's telling me that she'll use a fork and put it down and then go back to using a spoon. She's scared because using the fork ...' I couldn't continue. I was engulfed with emotion. I could feel Lilly's pain. I broke down and started crying my eyes out. Lilly was sending me signals by clairsentience and it was powerful stuff. 'She's so scared of growing up. She doesn't want to grow up. She's confused. You know when you say "you're my baby" and then you say "you're a big girl", because you do, don't you?' I was crying as I said this.

'Yes, that's correct.'

'Well, she's now totally confused.'

Then the reading went off on a tangent. I was shown a terrible event from Gemma's past. I was seeing this through the eyes of a child and it was very disturbing. I was flummoxed by this because it had come from literally nowhere. 'Totally nuts. I'd like to know about policemen,' I said.

'Pardon?' Gemma seemed really surprised by this comment.

'Handcuffs. Policemen?'

'Oh my God. I'd like to know a bit more.' Gemma seemed suddenly engrossed.

'Was someone arrested? Did someone get handcuffs put on them?'

'Yes.'

'Well this is worrying Lilly.' I decided to stop the reading. I'd said more than enough. I knew if I continued I would have to spend another two hours with Lilly and Gemma as there was so much information coming through. I felt I should wait until the home reading next

263

time. I was looking forward to seeing Gemma and Lilly again.

A few days later I was back in Chatham. I tried to tune in to Lilly and get myself into the zone before I entered her home, but for some reason I just couldn't. She kept blocking me. I hoped she'd open up when I sat with her and Gemma.

When I went into Gemma's lounge and sat down it was still really difficult to tune in to Lilly. Two pieces of information flashed before my third eye but I couldn't understand what they were. 'Lilly's telling me that you need to decorate a room. Do you understand this?' Gemma shrugged her shoulders. The information didn't seem to fit and I could see she was struggling to work out what it meant. Lilly then showed me an image of a girl or young woman and a boiling kettle. I wasn't sure what this meant so I just put two and two together and hoped they added up to four. 'Right, Gemma. I'm being told by Lilly that you seem to have a problem with Lilly scalding herself with boiling water, or did something happen to you with hot water when you were a kid? Do you remember this?'

'No.' I was surprised by Gemma's answer as this image seemed really powerful. Maybe I was subconsciously assuming this message to be something it wasn't. I didn't have time to think, though, as Lilly then showed me a house being broken into. It was scary and she'd been upset by it.

'There is also something coming through about a house being broken into. Do you understand that?'

'No.' I was stumped then. In my third eye I kept being shown three things: a girl or young woman, a kettle of boiling water and a house being broken into. I couldn't take these three images any further, and for 20 minutes we both sat staring at each other. There was something strange going on so I decided to take a break.

When I came back into the room after 10 minutes, Lilly suddenly began to talk to me telepathically. She started to tell me more things about herself and her life. 'Let's talk about bedtimes.' I knew Lilly wasn't sleeping because she kept showing me an image of her waking up in the middle of the night. 'Have you been locking the door or closing the door to Lilly's bedroom?'

'Closing the door,' replied Gemma, who by this point seemed slightly uninterested in the whole thing.

'Lilly's also telling me about the way she is sleeping. Does she get into bed with you?'

'She does.'

'I can see the way she sleeps when she's in bed with you. Would that be opposite to the way she sleeps in her own bed?'

'Yes.'

'Well, what we want to do is swap her bed round so that she's facing exactly the same direction she'd be facing if she was in your room.'

'Right.' Gemma smirked. I had the feeling she thought I was talking nonsense.

'And keep her bedroom door open and your bedroom door open so that she knows what's going on in your room and you'll have no more problems.'

Gemma didn't seem convinced. She nodded but I knew she didn't believe me.

For some reason Lilly was calmer now and was opening up to me. 'I'd like to talk about car seats,' I said. 'There seems to be a height issue. When Lilly sits on the sofa beside you she's at a low eye level to you. When she's in the car that eye level is different. It's higher than what she is used to because of the amount of foam in the car seat and it's freaking her out. She's absolutely scared shitless about going in the car. She needs a car seat that will allow her to have that low eye level, just like your sofa.'

'I'll do that,' said Gemma. I felt we were getting somewhere.

The next piece of information she sent me was about pushchairs. I was on a roll. 'When you take Gemma out in her pushchair, does she face you or face away from you?'

'Face away.'

'Have you noticed that the minute she gets in the pushchair she wants to get out?'

'Yes.' Gemma seemed impressed by my comment.

'Lilly needs to know that she is safe.' I'd come back to that later, though, as more and more information was starting to come through to me. 'Now I want you to involve Lilly more because she has just shown me you going to the shops with her, and she's said to me "I wish I could be part of the decision making". Now you probably think this is nuts but this is what she is saying. She needs that respect. This is why she is lashing out. Okay?'

'Okay.'

'Now this is weird. She's telling me about being scared and unsure of men.'

'Yes.'

'She's telling me about a man shouting, a man upsetting you, Gemma, a man shouting at you!'

'Yes.' I was touching a nerve and everyone in the room could feel it.

'When she's out in the street she can start screaming for no apparent reason because a man will go by or a man will scare her. Do you understand this?'

'I do.'

'Men – smartly dressed men – who pretend to be what they are not. Men who will smile and be nice to mum and then be horrible,' I punched my right fist into the palm of my left hand, 'and stab you right in the back! Who'll leave mum in bits and mum can't pull herself together and mum is a wreck!'

Gemma was now in a state. Tears were flowing down her cheeks. I had to continue though. Lilly wanted me to. 'The man who wants to touch mum's privates and bruise mum. The man who wants to bruise my mum!' By this time Gemma was sobbing her eyes out, but there was more from Lilly. '"Who the fuck are these men in my house?" she's saying. Lilly's swearing. These men came into the house and didn't say "Can we come into your house, Lilly?" These men just came into the house! I have had a problem today with being able to connect with Lilly because people didn't ask Lilly if it was alright.' I was beginning to get rather upset myself at this point. It was Lilly's way of releasing her anger and frustration at the world and she was letting everyone know about it. I'd never felt anger like this before from a child and it was an astounding tirade.

'Lilly knows that mum's been upset before by men and Lilly doesn't want mum to be upset by men again!' I exclaimed. 'And Lilly is freaked out about bruising, Gemma?'

'I understand bruises,' replied a very tearful Gemma.

'Leg bruises, Gemma?'

'Yes, I understand leg bruises.'

268

I had to stop. I couldn't take this anymore. I needed five minutes to disconnect from Lilly and get my head together. What I'd just been through was astounding. I could feel all of Lilly's pain and anger, and the pictures she was showing me of her mum's abuse were frightening.

I formulated a plan of action for Gemma to follow. I believed it would solve Lilly's behaviour problems and address her concerns. I went into the lounge and sat down with Gemma. I could see that she'd been crying since I'd left the room so I tried to be as calm as I could. 'You'll remember that Lilly was talking about car seats and how she kicks off when she gets into the car. So maybe it's worth thinking about getting a new car seat which will make her feel lower down?'

'Okay. The last thing I want to do is upset Lilly.'

'Lilly was also saying that she feels insecure in her pushchair. She wants to have a different type with a barrier around it. Lilly needs to know that you are there to protect her, Gemma. She also tells me that she would prefer to look at you rather than strangers when she's out and about.'

'Yes, that sounds like a good idea.'

'The next point is about involvement. Lilly wants to be a bigger part of your life. If you are cooking a meal, involve her with that and you will get a lot less hassle. Okay?'

'Okay.'

There were two more points I had to discuss with Gemma. First, I reiterated the need to change the direction of Lilly's bed. I was now at the last point in my plan. 'One of the biggest issues that came up, which was very upsetting for Lilly, was about men. I'm not a child expert or a child psychologist. Maybe, though, now is the time to start thinking about these issues.'

'I agree with what you are saying, Derek. I just want to help my daughter.'

'Gemma, it's up to you whether you act on the information that's come through in your reading and how you act on it, but whatever you do I wish you and Lilly the very best of luck.' I kissed Gemma and we hugged. It had been a very difficult reading, one that had started badly, but it had turned out to be one of the most dramatic readings I'd ever done. I knew there would be more to come the following week.

When I met with Lilly and Gemma seven days later it was much easier to connect with Lilly telepathically. 'She's fairly on the ball today, Gemma,' I said as I sat down on her sofa. 'How are you anyway?'

'I'm really good. Lilly's fine too.' I was pleased to hear it. Things were now beginning to come to me. I was being told more about Lilly's fears and her issues. I could feel the emotions welling up inside me. This was going to be difficult to talk about but I knew I had to do so.

'Now, let's go to the relationship with the man, the relationship that was sometimes okay but the majority of time was not good. Lilly is showing me blood on your bed. Do you understand what that means?'

'Yes.' For some reason I got the impression that Gemma knew I was going to bring this up.

'This has really affected Lilly, "Oh, the blood, the blood on the bed" she's telling me. Then there is a man coming into the house and mum is screaming. It's horrible. Oh my God! These images are scary, very scary for Lilly.'

Gemma looked shocked. I then kept being shown an image from Lilly that I remembered from the first reading but still didn't quite understand. She was constantly projecting a picture of a boiling kettle into my third eye. I could see the steam and the water bubbling. 'Lilly's showing me a kettle boiling. Is she trying to associate the fear of a boiling kettle with this other fear she's been talking about?'

'I used to say that my partner had a temper like a boiled kettle!' replied Gemma. Things were now beginning to fit. The jigsaw was coming together.

The reading was beginning to take on its own momentum. I started hearing voices, and the images Lilly was projecting to me were also getting more powerful and easier to understand. 'Now I'm hearing "Get your fucking bags packed. Get your fucking bags packed you bitch!"'

'Yes.'

'These are very strong words. Lilly has heard these words, and she's asking me to cry because these images are upsetting her. It's horrible. There is a lot of hitting going on in these images. I'm being shown a lot of bruises around your tummy.'

'Yes.' Gemma began to get upset. These memories were obviously still raw.

'I know this is horrendous for you. It's also horrendous for Lilly. Lilly doesn't know how she is going to handle it. Lilly is now saying to me "If I go to bed, Derek, is someone going to come in and hurt me? If I go to bed is someone going to come in and hurt mummy?" Yet again, this is the bed issue coming through. Lilly is telling me that when she is with you she can help you.' I stopped for a second. Lilly then asked me to do the strangest thing. She sent me a message telepathically to take off my jacket. I knew why she was doing this so I decided to share it with Gemma. 'I'm being asked to take my jacket off by Lilly.' Gemma started to laugh. I got the impression that she thought this was a ridiculous thing for her daughter to ask me. 'This is Lilly's way of saying to me that I'm now accepted in her home and that I'm no longer a threat to her or her mummy.'

I continued with the reading. 'I can hear the words "I'm fucking staying here. You can't throw me out" from the man who was here before and who hurt you. He took his jacket off when he said those things to you, but Lilly tells me that I can take mine off because I am welcome here.'

'That's totally correct,' replied Gemma. 'That happened.'

'Lilly is showing me that this man used to get very enraged and annoyed at you because you fucking didn't listen to him. She's telling me that he used to say to you "Who are you, you fucking idiot?", anything to make you feel belittled. In fact, Lilly has just shown me a rag doll. You were treated like a rag doll, Gemma, by your partner, the man who assaulted you.'

'That's right.'

There was more detail coming through. The images were getting stronger and more specific. 'Gemma, did your partner have a friend who was in prison? Who drove the car? Remember when they came that night and when they got out of the car they kept going on about the keys? I can hear from Lilly "Where are the fucking keys?" They seem to have lost keys? Do you remember?'

'Oh my God YES!'

'"Where are the fucking keys you fucking bitch?"'

'Yes!'

'Oh my God, Gemma.' I was overcome. These details were incredible. The way Lilly was now communicating with me was astounding. I felt I had to explain a few things to Gemma. 'I am so sorry for swearing. I'm sure some people would be shocked by this very strong language and wonder how it could be coming from a child like Lilly. Lilly doesn't know what the words mean. She is only repeating phrases that were said. Now Gemma, you need to deal with these issues. Once you have dealt with the relationship issue with this man, and also the dynamics of the relationship you have with Lilly, then Lilly will sleep. But not until then.'

When the reading was over, Gemma told me how much things had improved since the first reading. 'The improvements have been wonderful. I bought the car seat and the pram and both worked a treat. I've been involving Lilly in my daily chores and she's been responding really well. She now eats her dinner on her own and gives me peace to eat mine. I've been taking her out in the car and in her pram and she doesn't play up at all. This has been life changing for me.'

I was astounded by these results. 'I've made some notes about today and if it's okay I'd like to go over them. You need to allow time for yourself. When you take time out this will help Lilly and it will also help you.'

'Yes, I'd love to do that.' I could see from Gemma's expression that she was looking forward to having some time for herself, something she'd obviously been missing out on since her troubles began.

'The next point is about men.' Gemma laughed nervously. 'It's time to break the chains of that past relationship. Ultimately, it's up to you if you act on these points. I wish you every success. You deserve it.'

The day was over. It had been a hard slog full of emotions from the past. I was drained. I felt for Gemma. She'd obviously been through a great deal and those issues were still bothering her. More importantly, from my point of view, they were bothering Lilly too. That was out of my control, though. I was a baby mind reader and not a parent. I thought for a moment about what it would be like for me if I had my own child. I quickly got that notion out of my head. It was too scary for words!

A week later I arrived back in Chatham. Both Gemma and Lilly met me at the front door and looked pleased to see me. It was to be our last scheduled meeting. I was looking forward to it, though, because I knew Gemma would be conscientious enough to work through the notes I had left her with.

'So, Gemma, tell me how Lilly's behaviour is now?' I asked as we sat on Lilly's bed.

'I could never have imagined how happy I feel now and how different Lilly is. It's just amazing.' For the first time in weeks, Gemma looked like a mum who was in control of her life and, probably more importantly, of her child's life.

'I'm over the moon about that,' I replied.

I wanted to touch on some of the points that had come up in the readings. First, I asked Gemma about her issues with men. I was hoping she had made some positive steps.

'I'm making small changes every day,' she told me. 'Over the last week or so, I've started to give Lilly a lot more reassurance. I'm trying to change my attitude to what happened. It's hard. It's extremely hard, but we are trying, we are getting there.' I was so pleased to hear this news. I then asked Gemma about Lilly's sleeping patterns.

'I'm seeing a small improvement but not as dramatic as with the pushchair and the car seat. There is definitely an improvement, though.' Although I was slightly disappointed by this reply I knew that Lilly's sleeping problem had much to do with what Gemma had in her head, and this was something I couldn't control. Once Gemma had sorted out her past issues then – and only then – would Lilly sleep soundly in her bed at night.

My two weeks with Gemma and Lilly had passed. We had experienced the highs and also the lows but the results had been worth all the effort. I had achieved another goal and it was time for me to go home. There was a car waiting to take me to the airport. I'd be back in Kilbarchan in a few hours and I was looking forward to it. My time in Chatham was over and Bonnie Scotland was beckoning.

In many ways I feel that my life is just beginning. I've thought long and hard about what I've been through. Maybe everything that's happened to me has been for a reason. What if all the pain of my childhood and adolescence, my bankruptcy and my relationship with Michael had to occur to mould me into the person I am now? Perhaps I was born gay so that I could never have my own children and would develop an affinity with other people's children? There are so many questions I can't answer.

Looking back, I've had an amazing life. It's had its ups and downs but I've grown from each and every one of them. Sometimes it's been a huge fight but I've always managed to pull through and move on. I've learnt so much but probably my biggest lesson has been forgiveness. I really do now forgive everyone who did wrong to me and I wish them well.

When the sun sets in the sky and I sit with Casper, Beryl and Mo by my side, I'm thankful to God for small mercies. I feel more open and alive now and wonder if I can really make a difference. Maybe I'll inspire people to be a better version of what they already are. I've always been one for trying other avenues in life. Maybe now is the time to tap in to your sixth sense?